D1591964

Picturing Hemingway's Michigan

Picturing Hemingway's Michigan

Michael R. Federspiel

A Painted Turtle book

Detroit, Michigan

© 2010 by Wayne State University Press, Detroit, Michigan 48201.

All rights reserved. No part of this book may be reproduced without formal permission.

Manufactured in the United States of America.

14 13 12 11 10   5 4 3 2 1

Library of Congress Cataloging-in-Publication Data

Federspiel, Michael R.

Picturing Hemingway's Michigan / Michael R. Federspiel.

p. cm. — (Painted turtle books)

Includes bibliographical references and index.

ISBN 978-0-8143-3447-8 (cloth : alk. paper)

1. Hemingway, Ernest, 1899–1961—Homes and haunts—Michigan—Pictorial works. 2. Authors, American—Homes and haunts—Michigan—Pictorial works. 3. Literary landmarks—Michigan—Pictorial works. I. Title.

PS3515.E37Z589 2010

813'.52—dc22

[B]

2009037065

Designed and typeset by Maya Rhodes

Composed in Centaur MT, Avenir, and LHF Billhead 1900

*To my parents, **Ken and Nancy Federspiel**, who gave me the gift of Up North*

Contents

Preface ix

Introduction: Hemingway and Michigan xiii

1. "Up North" during Hemingway's Time, 1899–1921

The Tourist Industry 3

Great Lakes Steamships 8

Harbor Springs 19

Petoskey 23

Walloon Lake and Village 61

2. The Hemingway Family in Michigan

The Family 71

Windemere 81

Summers at the Cottage 93

3. Ernest's Michigan: Fact and Fiction

Ernest and Michigan 121

Fishing the Streams and Lakes 129

Hiking in Michigan 135

Horton Bay 140

Returning After the War 149

Seney and "Big Two-Hearted River" 159

Living in Petoskey, Fall 1919 171

Horton Bay Wedding 179

Epilogue 191

Bibliography 195

Permissions Acknowledgments 197

Index 199

PREFACE

In 2007 the Michigan Humanities Council created the Great Michigan Read program. This endeavor encouraged all Michiganians to read the same work and to talk about it. The council was determined to select an inaugural title that captured the essence of Michigan and would inspire programs and spirited discussions across the state. Its choice, Hemingway's *The Nick Adams Stories*, was both logical and inspired. (Over a span of two decades, Hemingway had written many short stories featuring the character Nick Adams that had been published in several different magazines and collections. In 1972 these were pulled together, arranged chronologically according to Nick's supposed age, and published in a single volume along with several previously unpublished fragments.) These stories about a young man's experiences in northern Michigan resonated with readers on many levels. Those who vacationed "Up North" recognized the places and emotions associated with getting away from home and experiencing the out-of-doors at a relaxed pace. Naturalists dwelled on the descriptions of turn-of-the-century Michigan, and fishermen (and fisherwomen) saw a fellow enthusiast in Nick. Students and teachers pondered the words and style that revolutionized American literature. And many more readers didn't worry about any literary concerns—they just liked the stories.

This work attempts to similarly do different things for different people. Those interested in the Little Traverse Bay region of northern Michigan will find information on that area between 1900 and 1920. It was a boom time that established an economy and way of life still in place today. People with a casual interest in Ernest Hemingway and his Michigan connections will find that story on these pages. They will meet the members of the Hemingway family, see how they were typical of thousands of other resorters, and learn about Ernest's early life. Those who bring to this work a solid knowledge of Hemingway's life and writing will find detailed evidence of the places, experiences, and people who inspired his writings.

The images in this book are drawn from a number of sources. Those of the region come from expected places—private collections, historical societies, archives, and libraries. But for the Hemingway images we must largely thank Ernest's parents, Clarence and Grace. Clarence was an avid and skilled photographer who began taking pictures in Michigan when he first visited there in 1898 with his wife and infant daughter, Marcelline. Over the next twenty-eight years he took countless photos of his family doing those things that all families do on vacation—playing in the water, fishing, boating, celebrating birthdays, and enjoying a family cottage. Using these images, Grace faithfully created multivolume scrapbooks for each of her children. Careful to treat them all equally, she had duplicate photos made that she pasted in along with her personal captions and comments. (It is from her, for example, that we know that Ernest is not shown in the group photo on his fifteenth birthday because he was fishing instead of socializing.) Ernest's five albums currently reside with his other personal papers at the John F. Kennedy Presidential Library in Boston, where they are cared for and made available to the public. Quotations in the text from these scrapbooks are taken, with thanks, from this source (JFK). Additionally, Michigan photos Ernest himself took are available there, and they provide the images of events that occurred when he was off on his own away from family.

In terms of specific thank-yous for support for this project, I am afraid the list is long and this space short. I owe so many people a debt of thanks for their help on either the local history or the Hemingway material. In particular, though, I would like to express my appreciation to the following.

The Michigan Hemingway Society has since the early 1990s publicized Ernest Hemingway's personal and literary connections to northern Michigan. This organization's outstanding board and members truly are the keepers of Hemingway's Michigan flame. By sponsoring a yearly conference and numerous initiatives, the society has informed countless people about this author's relationship to Michigan. The pioneering work of this organization has inspired and made it possible for me and others to understand Hemingway's connections to this state.

At the John F. Kennedy Presidential Library in Boston,

Hemingway archivist Susan Wrynn and Laurie Austin and James Hill in the audiovisual department were patient and generous with me and my endless requests for copies and access. Not only are they delightful people, they are doing excellent work in caring for some very special and fragile treasures.

The northern Michigan section would not have been possible without the support of the Little Traverse Regional Historical Society and Michelle Hill, its director. Its museum is housed on Petoskey's waterfront in the former Pere Marquette railroad depot and is a perfect place to start an area tour or to learn more about the rich history of the region. It has a permanent Hemingway exhibit and its photo collection is vast. I appreciate the access I was given to the museum resources and the support Ms. Hill provided to this whole project.

A special thanks goes to the Clarke Historical Library at Central Michigan University and its director, Frank Boles. Dr. Boles has been personally and professionally supportive and I value his friendship and expertise. I also appreciate the many hours Pat Thelen, the library's scanning technician, put in to make many of this book's images possible. The Clarke Library is the premiere location for research on Hemingway's Michigan connections and the Great Lakes region's history. It houses a substantial Hemingway collection, including several original letters written by him that reference Michigan. Quotations from Hemingway's letters in the text not otherwise attributed are reprinted, with gratitude, from this source (CMU). It also oversees the Michigan Hemingway Endowment, to which the author's profits from this work will be donated. The endowment supports the purchase of Hemingway-related materials and sponsors activities designed to increase knowledge of his relationship with this state.

Finally, my most heartfelt thanks go to Jim and Marian Sanford. Without their support, the Hemingway sections of the book would not have been as rich or comprehensive. Jim's mother was Marcelline Hemingway Sanford (Ernest's older sister), and he is a careful and generous overseer of his family's legacy. His friendship and support are greatly valued and appreciated.

INTRODUCTION

∽ HEMINGWAY AND MICHIGAN

Ernest Hemingway's connections to Michigan began when his parents first brought their six-week-old son there for three days in September 1899. His father, a young physician, practiced medicine in his hometown of Oak Park, Illinois, and his mother was an artistically inclined woman who enjoyed the cultural aspects of their Chicago suburb. The previous summer the Hemingways visited Walloon Lake (then named Bear Lake) and were so taken with the area that they purchased two hundred feet of waterfront property. The 1899 trip was to finalize plans for the building of their cottage, Windemere. They took pictures, selected the exact site on the property where it was to be located, and arranged for construction during their brief stay. The next summer would be the first full one there for the family, and Ernest would return to Michigan each year until he was married in 1921. Even today members of the Hemingway family either summer or live year-round in the area.

The Hemingways' arrival coincided with dramatic changes in northern Michigan. A generation earlier, lumber companies cleared most of the virgin timber and then moved on, leaving a handful of small villages and thousands of acres of abandoned land behind. What would become of that land was in question. In an effort to encourage people to settle there, railroad companies were given large land grants in exchange for extending rail lines northward from the larger cities in the southern parts of the state. This included the Grand Rapids and Indiana (GR & I), which received a grant of 823,204 acres in 1857 to institute rail service between Grand Rapids and "some point on Traverse Bay." When the company finished laying tracks to Petoskey in 1873, local businessmen and railroad executives immediately went to work marketing the region for tourism. The locals knew that tourists would need to be housed, fed, and entertained, while railroad officials knew they could make money transporting both passengers and freight to and from the northland. Additionally, they could profit from selling land they had been granted and by partnering with resort hotels. More growth in the region meant more profit. Simultaneously, steamship companies knew that by adding passenger service to their existing freight service they too could capitalize on the new boom. In the absence of rail lines and roads, the Great Lakes steamship companies had been calling on local ports for decades and had been the primary carriers of goods to and from the north. With adjustments to existing ships and the purchase of new passenger ships they could promote both the journey and the destinations. The steamship and railroad companies both mounted elaborate and effective marketing campaigns that brought travelers from as far away as St. Louis, Kansas City, and Louisville. Tourists were lured by the pure northern air, the natural beauty of the lakes and forests, and the potential to enjoy either a leisurely or an active experience. Local excursions were developed both for those who wanted just to look at nature from afar and for those who wanted to experience it through hiking, hunting, and fishing.

The impact on the region was immediate and profound. When the railroad came to Petoskey in 1873, two families lived there; by 1900, its population was just over six thousand. At its peak there were thirteen resort hotels in Petoskey alone (positioning it as a main competitor to Mackinac Island as the premiere destination in northern Michigan) and numerous other resorts and associations scattered along the edge of Little Traverse Bay. These included Bay View, a Methodist summer meeting place established in 1875 and made possible by local businessmen and railroad officials securing property for the site. An elaborate regional rail network made travel convenient, while local merchants were poised to meet the needs and wants of their summer guests. This transformation had long-standing effects, as even today many of the same patterns and practices are in place.

The Hemingways, when they bought property at Walloon Lake in 1898, were just one of hundreds of families who were flocking to the region. They would experience and enjoy the area and its people the way countless others did. Choosing to be cottage owners rather than stay at the large resorts, they traveled on ships and trains and enjoyed their Walloon Lake community and trips to and through towns such as Petoskey, Harbor Springs, and Charlevoix. There was nothing particularly unusual or noteworthy about the family. They resembled others in their lifestyle and background, and there was little to indicate anything special about them.

Today, however, the name Ernest Hemingway immediately brings to mind an internationally known writer, legendary drinker, big-game hunter, and deep-sea fisherman. But between 1899 and 1921—his Michigan years—there was little to suggest that he would become famous. He was then just another young man who summered Up North with his family. While a host of factors resulted in his successful writing and fame, northern Michigan did play an important role in his life—both personally and professionally. Personally, it provided prolonged exposure to the natural world and to places and people that, to him, were exotic and far removed from his respectable middle-class life in Oak Park. There he was a good student growing up in a highly structured but creative household. His mother exposed him to the arts and his father to the sciences and the natural world. Exciting places

and adventures were experienced through reading and his vivid imagination. But come summer, his life changed dramatically. Via steamship and train he was transported to a whole different world and situation. Northern Michigan was not where you read about nature, it was where you lived with and in it. It was a place where bare feet replaced shoes and where the sounds you heard at night were the wind and birds, not the hum of a Chicago suburb. Hot and muggy city nights gave way to cool evenings requiring covers pulled up tight. Michigan was also a place of local color where real "Indians" lived and where the legacy of the wild lumber era was still palpable. And, especially for Ernest, it was a place of solitude. Throughout his life he needed and sought private time to think and contemplate. In Michigan's forests and streams he spent hours—very often alone—observing and experiencing. He also found friends and an audience in Michigan. True, they were most often other "summer people" rather than the locals who lived there year-round, but they were friends with whom he shared stories, laughs, and experiences unlike those in Oak Park.

Professionally, Michigan supplied Hemingway with the setting and characters for his formative writing. As he struggled to find his style and themes in the 1920s, he focused on what he knew well—the people and places of his summers. Sitting in cafés in Paris, he sifted through his memories and carefully selected actual people and places for inspiration. It is tempting to look at his final product and to think that Hemingway wrote things just as they happened, but he tells us this is not true and we should believe him. He pulled the essence from Michigan and created something all new. During the 1920s and 1930s he wrote and published stories featuring Nick Adams, a young man who just happens to spend summers in northern Michigan with his doctor father and artistic mother. Nick also just happens to have been wounded in World War I and loves to fish and spend time with friends around Horton Bay and Petoskey.

It is true that Hemingway used his own life experiences as a starting point for his fiction, but Nick Adams is not Ernest Hemingway, despite their commonalities. In addition to the Nick Adams stories, Hemingway's first published novel, *The Torrents of Spring*, is set in Michigan. While it contains some wonderful descriptions of Petoskey and the surrounding area, for the most part it is an unsatisfying satire that did little more than allow him to break a publishing contract. But still, it is Hemingway using his Michigan for inspiration. Peppered through his later works are references to Michigan, and it is especially telling that his late-in-life account of Paris in the 1920s, *A Moveable Feast*, has numerous references to Michigan. Clearly, even though he physically left Michigan behind, he continued to be inspired by it for the rest of his life.

I

"Up North" during Hemingway's Time, 1899–1921

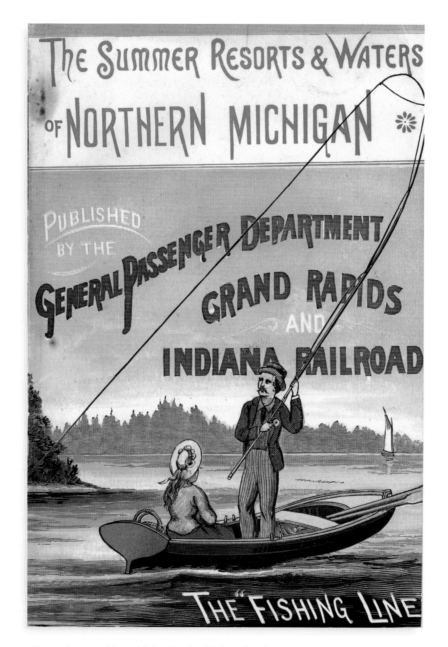

Promotional booklet published by the GR & I railroad company, ca. 1886. (Courtesy of Clarke Historical Library, Central Michigan University, Mount Pleasant.)

THE TOURIST INDUSTRY

The Hemingways' initial decision to buy property in northern Michigan rather than some other location was not happenstance. Undoubtedly they, like thousands of others, became aware of the region through an aggressive and effective marketing campaign sponsored by railroad and steamship companies and by the Petoskey community itself.

FARMING IN MICHIGAN

Michigan offers among other things; good soil of all types; healthful climate; natural drainage; adequate rainfall; good local markets; good schools and churches; good roads, opportunities for stock raising; fruit growing; dairying; general farming; market gardening; seed growing; poultry and bee raising, etc., and ranks first and second in the production of many staple crops.

The Grand Rapids & Indiana Railway has recently established demonstration farms at five points along its line in Northern Michigan for giving material assistance to farmers and new settlers.

For detail information regarding available farm lands, crops, markets, homeseekers' fares, etc., write

W. P. Hartman,
Agricultural & Industrial Agent,
G. R. & I. R'y.,
Grand Rapids, Mich.

In addition to tourists, the railroads targeted farmers in their promotional publications. (Courtesy of Clarke Historical Library, Central Michigan University, Mount Pleasant.)

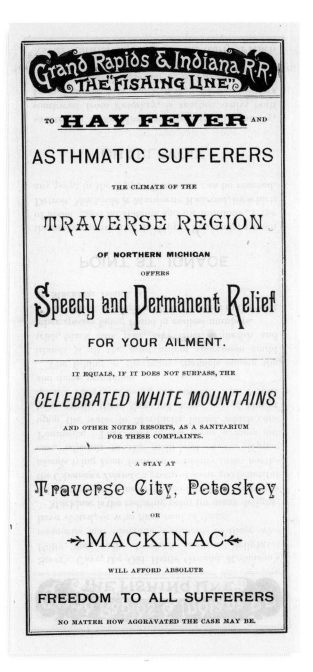

GR & I promotional booklet, 1870. (Courtesy of Clarke Historical Library, Central Michigan University, Mount Pleasant.)

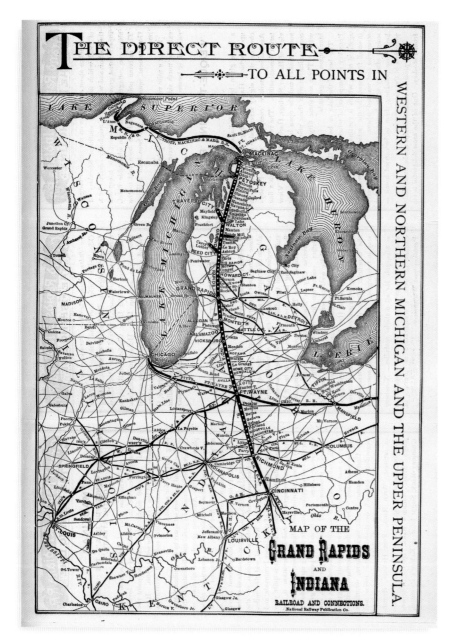

Locally produced publications also encouraged tourists.
(Courtesy of Clarke Historical Library, Central Michigan University, Mount Pleasant.)

GR & I route map showing how easy it was to get to Petoskey and other points north from most midwestern cities. (Courtesy of Clarke Historical Library, Central Michigan University, Mount Pleasant.)

A group of turn-of-the-century tourists in Petoskey. (Courtesy of Little Traverse Region Historical Museum, Petoskey.)

I might tell you of the thousands of charming people we met, of the fact, that almost without exception, they were as enthusiastic as I am, as to the unequaled beauty and utility of Northern Michigan for summer visitors or winter huntsmen—and how all, or at least nearly all—who had hay fever, asthma, or other bronchial or lung difficulties, or were victims of malaria before their arrival, were cured, made good as new, to the comforts of their bodies, and the depletion of their bank account— because such voracious eaters must pay a little something for what they devour!

Anon., *Summer Resorts and Waters of Northern Michigan* (1884), 8.

The Hemingway children in Petoskey on their way home from northern Michigan, August 1906. Left to right: Ernest, Marcelline, Madelaine, and Ursula. (Courtesy of the Ernest Hemingway Collection at the John F. Kennedy Presidential Library, Boston.)

The Northern Michigan Transportation Company's 1916 publication showed the *Manitou* on its cover. (Courtesy of Clarke Historical Library, Central Michigan University, Mount Pleasant.)

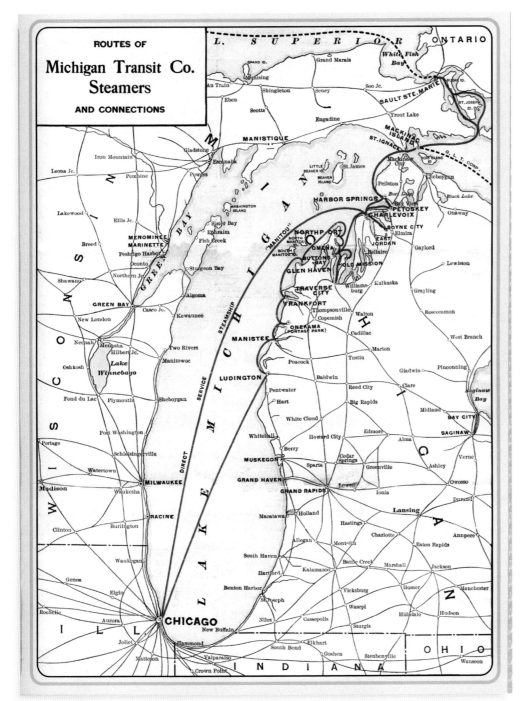

The Michigan Transit Company's routes were shown in its 1921 advertising booklet. (Author's collection.)

BOAT LANDING NEAR EAST END MUNICIPAL PIER, CHICAGO

Countless people escaped hot Chicago summers for northern Michigan each year. (Author's collection.)

GREAT LAKES STEAMSHIPS

Between 1900 and 1920 railroad and steamship companies competed fiercely for tourists' patronage. Initially, the steamships had an advantage as they had been dealing with northern Michigan lakeside communities for decades. In the absence of roads or rail lines, goods had to be shipped to and from residents along Michigan's coast by water. When the railroads arrived and tourism began to boom, the steamship companies shifted their focus.

The Northern Michigan Transportation Company invested in impressive and comfortable steamships and advertised excursions to Michigan that included either long- or short-term stops at destinations including Mackinac Island and Petoskey, where hotels and entertainment awaited the passengers. Chicago was a particularly heavily targeted city, and its newspapers often included tempting advertisements. By the end of the 1920s, passenger service had largely died out because of automobiles and improved roads. But in their heyday, steamships afforded passengers an opportunity to travel in comfort and style.

STEAMSHIP MANITOU

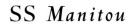

Left: The *Manitou* about to dock at Harbor Springs. (Author's collection.)

Bottom: The *Manitou* leaving Charlevoix. (Courtesy of Clarke Historical Library, Central Michigan University, Mount Pleasant.)

SS *Manitou*

For many years the SS *Manitou* was the queen of the Great Lakes, known for speed and luxury. Built in 1893, it was 274 feet long and 42 feet wide and typically made the Chicago to Mackinac run three times a week, stopping at several ports along the way, including Harbor Springs. The Hemingways were passengers several times, including in September 1899 when the infant Ernest made his first trip to northern Michigan.

Copyright 1905 by the Rotograph Co.

A 7514 S. S. Manitou, leaving the Canal, Charlevoix, Mich.

Chicago newspaper advertisement for the *Manitou*, 1903. (Courtesy of Clarke Historical Library, Central Michigan University, Mount Pleasant.)

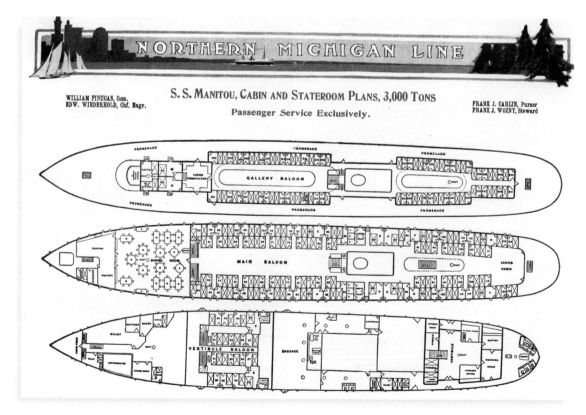

Manitou deck plans, 1916. (Courtesy of Clarke Historical Library, Central Michigan University, Mount Pleasant.)

Dr. Clarence Hemingway aboard the *Manitou*, 1920s. (Courtesy of the Ernest Hemingway Collection at the John F. Kennedy Presidential Library, Boston.)

MICHIGAN TRANSIT CO.

S.S. MANITOU | *CABIN TICKET*

Good between punches

ROOM $\left\{\begin{array}{l} \text{U} \underline{\hspace{3cm}} \\ \text{L} \underline{\hspace{3cm}} \end{array}\right.$

GLEN HAVEN ★
CHARLEVOIX ★
PETOSKEY ★
HARBOR SPGS. ★
MACKINAC ISLD. ★

Only on T stamped on Back.

IMPORTANT
MUST BE PRESENTED TO COLLECTOR TO GAIN ADMISSION TO CABIN

HAND TO COLLECTOR AS YOU LEAVE STEAMER

Kennedy
Gen'l Pass'r Agt

5158

Manitou ticket. (Courtesy of Clarke Historical Library, Central Michigan University, Mount Pleasant.)

The *Manitou* docking at Harbor Springs with bay ferry steamer *Columbia* in foreground. (Courtesy of Little Traverse Region Historical Museum, Petoskey.)

SS *Missouri*

Ernest Hemingway was very familiar with the SS *Missouri.* It was smaller than the *Manitou,* only 225 feet long, but it could transport 250 passengers and fifteen hundred tons of cargo. Built in 1899, it was owned by the Michigan Transportation Company between 1904 and 1918. This vessel carried Ernest from Chicago on his hiking trips in 1915 and 1916. It also made stops around Lake Charlevoix, pausing at Horton Bay where it picked up fruits and vegetables grown on the Hemingway farm for shipment back to them in Oak Park, Illinois.

STEAMSHIP "MISSOURI" IN RIVER AT CHARLEVOIX, MICH.

The *Missouri* was active on both Lake Michigan and Lake Charlevoix, on which Horton Bay was located. (Author's collection.)

The *Missouri* transported people, freight, and mail. (Courtesy of Clarke Historical Library, Central Michigan University, Mount Pleasant.)

Ernest Hemingway aboard the *Missouri*, ca. 1916. (Courtesy of the Ernest Hemingway Collection at the John F. Kennedy Presidential Library, Boston.)

Bay Ferries

Local residents and tourists used ferries to travel around Little
Traverse Bay. These smaller steamers stopped at resort communities
and towns and transported both goods and people to destinations
larger steamships did not serve. While the Hemingways would not
have availed themselves of them regularly, these steamers provided
timely service to those arriving or departing by train or the larger
Great Lakes steamships.

Nº304   LITTLE TRAVERSE BAY FERRY STEAMERS 'SILVER SPRAY' AND "SEARCH LIGHT."

The *Search Light* and the *Silver Spray* provided
service to Harbor Springs, Bay View, Petoskey,
and Charlevoix. (Author's collection.)

View of Little Traverse Bay and the Bay View dock. (Courtesy of Little Traverse Region Historical Museum, Petoskey.)

Wequetonsing residents had traditionally relied on boat and rail service, but eventually roads like the one shown here were improved as automobiles became the preferred mode of travel. (Courtesy of Little Traverse Region Historical Museum, Petoskey.)

View of Little Traverse Bay from Bay View. (Courtesy of Little Traverse Region Historical Museum, Petoskey.)

The *Vernon* not only served Little Traverse Bay but also made runs to Chicago. In 1887 it was caught in a severe gale and sank in Lake Michigan, with only one of the fifty people on board saved. (Courtesy of Little Traverse Region Historical Museum, Petoskey.)

The *Gazelle* at the Petoskey dock. Notice the antlers affixed atop the pilothouse. (Courtesy of Little Traverse Region Historical Museum, Petoskey.)

HARBOR SPRINGS

Originally named Little Traverse, Harbor Springs benefited from tourism and from the services of the railroads and steamship companies. The rapid growth and popularity of resort communities brought activity and prosperity to the town. Its natural deep harbor made it ideal for larger vessels like the *Northland* and the *Manitou.* Rail service reached Harbor Springs in 1881, and the depot was built the following year. By 1906 its business district had expanded to approximately its current boundaries. Harbor Springs was where the Hemingway family typically disembarked from their steamship and oversaw the loading of their trunks and baggage onto a train for the trip around the bay to Petoskey.

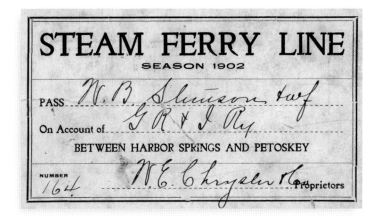

Little Traverse Bay steam ferry ticket, 1902. (Courtesy of Little Traverse Region Historical Museum, Petoskey.)

Harbor Springs was blessed with an excellent deep natural harbor that made it perfect as a port. The village is in the foreground, Harbor Point in the distance. (Courtesy of Little Traverse Region Historical Museum, Petoskey.)

Top: The SS *Manitou* passing the lighthouse at Harbor Point in 1908. (Courtesy of Little Traverse Region Historical Museum, Petoskey.)

Bottom: Busy Harbor Springs harbor, with the *Northland* departing as the *Manitou* waits to dock. One of the bay ferries is already at the dock. (Courtesy of Little Traverse Region Historical Museum, Petoskey.)

A12—VIEW OF BUSINESS SECTION AND BAY, HARBOR SPRINGS, MICH.

No. 53. State Street, Harbor Springs, Mich.

Top: Harbor Springs, looking south along State Street. (Courtesy of Little Traverse Region Historical Museum, Petoskey.)

Bottom: Harbor Spring's State Street has changed little over the years. (Courtesy of Little Traverse Region Historical Museum, Petoskey.)

The Harbor Springs depot where the Hemingways would have boarded a train with their luggage bound for the GR & I station at Petoskey. This depot still stands. (Courtesy of Clarke Historical Library, Central Michigan University, Mount Pleasant.)

Trains ran regularly between Petoskey and Harbor Springs with stops at resort communities along the way. (Courtesy of Little Traverse Region Historical Museum, Petoskey.)

Souvenir postcards for tourists were and are popular in Petoskey. (Author's collection.)

PETOSKEY

During Ernest Hemingway's Michigan years, Petoskey was the Little Traverse region's main city. A sleepy little village until rail service arrived in 1873, its population was over six thousand by 1900, when it boasted two newspapers, an expanding business district, impressive hotels, and an industrial area with lumber mills and pump manufacturing. Additionally, it was a transportation hub, with dozens of trains and ships arriving and departing daily. Hemingway would use it as a setting for his first published novel, *The Torrents of Spring,* and it was his residence for several weeks in the fall of 1919.

Railroads

GRAND RAPIDS AND INDIANA

The arrival of the Grand Rapids and Indiana Railroad to Petoskey transformed the region from one of lumbermen and Native Americans to one whose economy and reputation were based on tourism. In the years after the Civil War, the GR & I gradually pushed rail lines north, taking advantage of land grants and communities' desires to have access to railroads for transportation of people and goods. The last stretch from Fife Lake to Petoskey was completed in 1873, with passenger service beginning the next year. Recognizing the profit potential, the GR & I immediately began marketing the region as a tourist destination. Dubbing itself as "The Fishing Line," it began publishing elaborate booklets describing the attractions of the Little Traverse Bay area. These publications (as well as newspaper advertisements) targeted audiences in the midwestern cities served by the railroad. As a result, readers in St. Louis, Louisville, and Kansas City began to

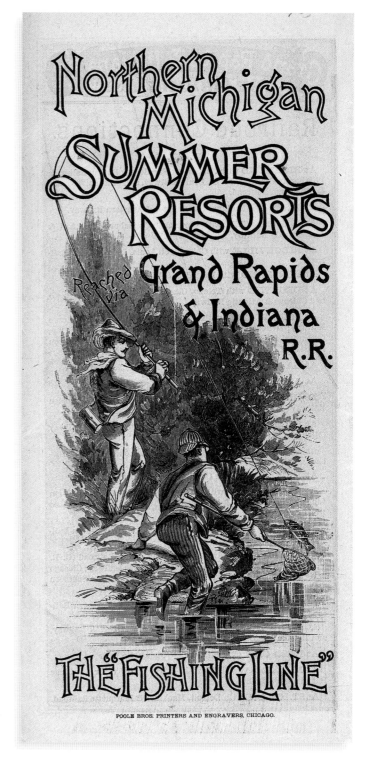

GR & I promotional booklet, 1870.
(Courtesy of Clarke Historical Library, Central Michigan University, Mount Pleasant.)

consider escaping the summer heat and traveling to Michigan for a quick getaway or a longer vacation. The publications described the natural beauty of water and woods, the healthy northern climate, the sporting opportunities, and the world-class accommodations available at the new majestic hotels. Initially tourists came almost exclusively to stay at these large resort hotels, where all the cultural opportunities and comforts they expected were available, but soon a different kind of "tourist" emerged. With the establishment of Bay View, a Methodist camp on the edge of Petoskey in 1875, the annual "resorter" emerged alongside the more transient vacationer. Resort communities such as Wequetonsing, Roaring Brook, Menoniqua Beach, and Harbor Point were established around Little

Top: Trains ran regularly between Petoskey and Harbor Springs with stops at resort communities along the way. (Courtesy of Little Traverse Region Historical Museum, Petoskey.)

Bottom: The We Que Ton Sing station was one of several along Little Traverse Bay. (Courtesy of Little Traverse Region Historical Museum, Petoskey.)

Traverse Bay and began to welcome hundreds of the same families back each year—much to the delight of the railroad owners who profited by hauling them and their supplies.

GR & I Main Station ∽ The Grand Rapids and Indiana Railroad Company's connection to Petoskey was essential to the economic development of the region. The main station received trains year-round from all around the Midwest, including the Northland Limited Express, which brought with it sleeper cars and passengers from as far away as St. Louis, Cincinnati, and Louisville. This station still stands and is located at the intersection of Bay and Lewis streets.

The Northland Limited transported thousands each year to and from northern Michigan. (Courtesy of Little Traverse Region Historical Museum, Petoskey.)

The Grand Rapids and Indiana Railroad station in Petoskey with the Arlington Hotel in the distance. (Courtesy of Little Traverse Region Historical Museum, Petoskey.)

The GR & I lines for the dummy and long-haul trains ran through the center of Petoskey. Lake Street is visible here, as is the main station in the background. The Cushman Hotel is to the right. Today this area is Pennsylvania Park. (Courtesy of Little Traverse Region Historical Museum, Petoskey.)

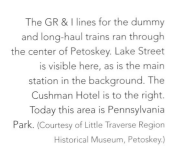

At right: Luggage, especially for those staying long term, was always plentiful at the rail stations. The Hemingways would have brought clothes and essentials for a three-month stay. This image was taken at the Petoskey GR & I suburban station. (Courtesy of Little Traverse Region Historical Museum, Petoskey.)

Far right: A GR & I timetable publication for fall 1915. (Courtesy of Clarke Historical Library, Central Michigan University, Mount Pleasant.)

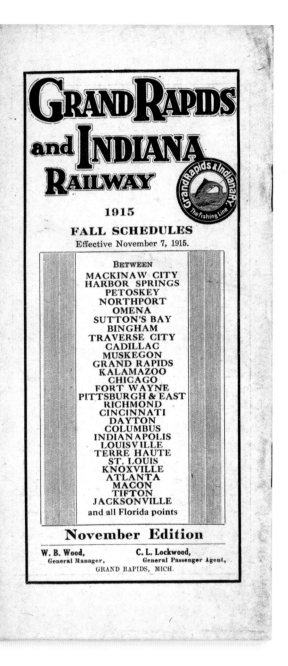

GRAND RAPIDS and INDIANA RAILWAY

Grand Rapids & Indiana Ry.
The Fishing Line

1915

FALL SCHEDULES

Effective November 7, 1915.

BETWEEN
MACKINAW CITY
HARBOR SPRINGS
PETOSKEY
NORTHPORT
OMENA
SUTTON'S BAY
BINGHAM
TRAVERSE CITY
CADILLAC
MUSKEGON
GRAND RAPIDS
KALAMAZOO
CHICAGO
FORT WAYNE
PITTSBURGH & EAST
RICHMOND
CINCINNATI
DAYTON
COLUMBUS
INDIANAPOLIS
LOUISVILLE
TERRE HAUTE
ST. LOUIS
KNOXVILLE
ATLANTA
MACON
TIFTON
JACKSONVILLE
and all Florida points

November Edition

W. B. Wood,
General Manager,

C. L. Lockwood,
General Passenger Agent,
GRAND RAPIDS, MICH.

Night in Petoskey. Long past midnight. Inside the beanery a light burning. The town asleep under the Northern moon. To the North the tracks of the GR & I Railroad running far into the North. Cold tracks stretching North toward Mackinac City and St. Ignace. Cold tracks to be walking at this time of night. . . . On they stride. Into the North. Into the Northern night.

Torrents of Spring, 87.

Suburban or "Summer" Station ⤫ In addition to those trains arriving from points distant, there was also an elaborate network of "dummy trains" that provided local service. So named because they did not really go anywhere other than to and from the small local resort stops, these suburban trains nonetheless provided regular and essential daily transportation for goods and people. During the summer, a special suburban station was opened and used for the dummy trains. It was located a block from the main station on Lake Street (across the street from the Cushman Hotel) and was a popular gathering spot. When they arrived in Petoskey, people like the Hemingways would have used this station and dummy trains to get to their final destination. Once settled in, they would continue to use the dummies all summer long to travel the region. At the peak of the season, trains ran every fifteen to thirty minutes, and an August 1885 newspaper article reported that an estimated eight thousand fares were collected between Bay View and Petoskey alone on a particularly busy weekend.

The dummy trains typically had two or three coaches, with one partitioned to provide areas for baggage and a men's smoking car.

They had back-to-back wooden benches, and one rider reported that the floors were painted red and the rest of the interior gray. A conductor was responsible for upkeep of the coaches and collecting fares. It was quite common for shoppers to leave their resort communities for a day of shopping in Petoskey, taking with them large expandable bags to fill with their purchases. The train cars were often completely filled with people and goods at the end of the day, and it was common to see several people eating popcorn purchased in Petoskey. With the advent of automobiles and improved roads, however, the dummy trains were in less and less demand; by 1921 typically only one ran to resorts per day, and by 1925 dummy service was discontinued altogether.

The first GR & I dummy train in Petoskey, 1876. (Courtesy of Little Traverse Region Historical Museum, Petoskey.)

A typical suburban train in the Little Traverse region. (Courtesy of Little Traverse Region Historical Museum, Petoskey.)

The suburban dummy train station on Lake Street. This station was open only during the summer season. The location is currently the parking lot adjacent to the Emmet County Building on Lake Street across from the City Park Grill. (Courtesy of Little Traverse Region Historical Museum, Petoskey.)

No.309 G.R. & I. SUBURBAN STATION, PETOSKEY, MICH.

ALTON G.COOK, PUBL. PETOSKEY, MICH.

View of the main GR & I station showing a regular and dummy train side by side. Notice the difference in engines and cars. The location of the house in the background is approximately where the Hotel Perry was built in 1899. (Courtesy of Little Traverse Region Historical Museum, Petoskey.)

The station was a social as well as a transportation center with trains departing every fifteen minutes in the peak of the season. (Author's collection.)

Railroad staff would have been busy serving hundreds of passengers on busy days. (Courtesy of Little Traverse Region Historical Museum, Petoskey.)

G.R+I Sub. Station Force 1915

Suburban station with Lake Street and the Cushman Hotel in the background. (Courtesy of Clarke Historical Library, Central Michigan University, Mount Pleasant.)

SUBURBAN STATION AND TRAINS, PETOSKEY, MICH.

G. R. & I. NORTHLAND LIMITED AND SUBURBAN TRAINS, PETOSKEY, MICHIGAN

Eventually a metal pedestrian crosswalk was built over the tracks to help passengers get safely from the main to the suburban station. (Courtesy of Clarke Historical Library, Central Michigan University, Mount Pleasant.)

Hotels

Working in tandem with the steamship and railroad companies, local business leaders constructed and operated hotels to encourage and then to accommodate the growing number of summer tourists. At its peak, Petoskey boasted over a dozen first-class, full-service hotels and numerous small guesthouses and boardinghouses. The major ones, such as the Arlington and the Cushman, provided the level of service and entertainment one would expect at any luxury resort in the country. This included in-house orchestras, fine dining, day excursions, and ornate public and private rooms.

The Cushman

The Cushman House Hotel, originally built by David Cushman in 1875, would eventually extend from Lake Street to Mitchell Street on the east side of Railroad Park (today Pennsylvania Park). After it opened, the hotel underwent a number of changes, chief among them the addition of a 254-foot porch with Ionic columns in 1899. In 1901 a brick annex was added that faced Mitchell Street and housed fifty additional guest rooms and a post office on the ground floor. Capacity of the hotel was 350 guests who could enjoy the Cushman House orchestra daily: the lunch recital at 11:00 a.m., the afternoon tea dance, and dancing in the evening. Unlike most of its rivals, the Cushman stayed open in the winter, making it a year-round social center. Ernest Hemingway stayed here in September 1919 when he arrived in Petoskey to begin an extended stay. The annex eventually was heavily damaged by a fire, and the main hotel fell into disrepair and was sold and torn down in the 1930s.

The Cushman House Hotel before it was redone in 1899 to include the elaborate columns and porch. Note the evolving roofline above the lobby door. (Courtesy of Little Traverse Region Historical Museum, Petoskey.)

The Cushman with what is today the City Park Grill visible through the welcome arch on Lake Street. (Courtesy of Little Traverse Region Historical Museum, Petoskey.)

Cushman Hotel, Petoskey, Mich.

The Cushman after the 1899 renovations, ca. 1920. (Courtesy of Clarke Historical Library, Central Michigan University, Mount Pleasant.)

The Cushman orchestra playing in the adjacent park (today known as Pennsylvania Park). Appropriately, a public bandstand currently stands in this location. (Courtesy of Little Traverse Region Historical Museum, Petoskey.)

Drawing of the Cushman taken from an early menu. (Courtesy of Little Traverse Region Historical Museum, Petoskey.)

The Cushman's porch was a popular gathering spot. (Courtesy of Little Traverse Region Historical Museum, Petoskey.)

The Arlington

The Arlington, Petoskey's most famous and impressive hotel, actually had two distinct lives. The original Arlington cost $60,000 when it was built in 1882 by Hiram Rose, a Petoskey businessman, and was located immediately adjacent to the GR & I rail tracks and station. It was four stories high and could accommodate three hundred guests in its 115 rooms. Rooms were furnished with carpets and black walnut, cherry, or ash bedroom suites with marble tops. Guests could enjoy the house orchestra in the basement dance hall, the forty-by-seventy-foot dining room with its staff of twenty-two "colored" waiters, two billiard halls (one for men and the other for women), a bar, barbershop, and reception room with velvet carpets. If patrons wanted time away from their children, attended indoor and outdoor play areas were available, as was a nursery. From the twelve-foot-wide veranda, guests enjoyed a view of the "million-dollar" sunsets that took place every night.

The Arlington Hotel. Note how close it was to the railroad tracks. (Courtesy of Little Traverse Region Historical Museum, Petoskey.)

So successful was the Arlington that it received a major renovation and was reopened as the New Arlington on July 4, 1901. With three hundred rooms (plus thirty-six suites with bathrooms and toilets) and a capacity of eight hundred, this hotel rivaled Mackinac Island's Grand Hotel as the premiere lodging in northern Michigan. Added were an additional floor, elevators, steam heat, and a twenty-four-foot veranda around the entire building. The dining

The New Arlington Hotel. (Courtesy of Little Traverse Region Historical Museum, Petoskey.)

When the New Arlington burned in June 1915, the heat was so intense that it warped the railroad tracks running beside the hotel. (Courtesy of Little Traverse Region Historical Museum, Petoskey.)

hall was enlarged to 65 by 125 feet, and guests especially enjoyed Ping-Pong tables in the lobby. Searchlights mounted on the veranda roof illuminated the night sky and cityscape. Diners feasted on meals prepared by French chefs, including stewed or raw oysters, lamb, duck, and prime rib. Sadly, the structure burned on July 19, 1915, and newly enacted fire codes that prohibited the construction of wooden hotels made it impossible for the owners to rebuild. Today the site is the home of Arlington Park.

Advertisement for the New Arlington, ca. 1912. (Courtesy of Little Traverse Region Historical Museum, Petoskey.)

New Arlington Hotel

EUROPEAN

S. H. PECK, PROPRIETOR

The New Arlington Hotel, Petoskey, Mich.

PETOSKEY'S CLASSY

HOTEL AND GRILL

Sea Foods and all the Land offers--appealing to the people who are looking for something good to eat and first-class service. . . . . .

Finest Orchestra in North Michigan
MUSIC DAILY AND EVENINGS

THE PERRY

The Hotel Perry (now known as the Perry Hotel) was built the year Ernest Hemingway was born (1899) and was constructed of brick—a response to fire hazards and fears. A medium-size hotel, it originally could accommodate 150 guests. In 1919 it was sold with the intention of converting it to a hospital. Intervention by city leaders convinced the new owners, Drs. John and George Reycroft, to retain it as a hotel. The last of the great hotels in existence, it is still in operation and welcomes guests to stay or dine each year. Its location immediately across the street from the main GR & I station helped it solicit lodgers—including a young Ernest Hemingway, who spent 75¢ for a room there in 1916.

Advertisement for the Hotel Perry, ca. 1905. (Courtesy of Clarke Historical Library, Central Michigan University, Mount Pleasant.)

HOTEL PERRY, PETOSKEY

The Hotel Perry before and after (1928) an addition.
(Courtesy of Little Traverse Region Historical Museum, Petoskey.)

The Hotel Perry with the GR & I station and pedestrian rail crosswalk in the foreground. (Courtesy of Little
Traverse Region Historical Museum, Petoskey.)

Other Hotels

In addition to the major hotels, smaller ones such as the Park,

Clifton, Oriental, and National also welcomed visitors to Petoskey.

Less sophisticated than the resort hotels, they nonetheless provided

comfortable and more moderately priced lodgings.

The Park House, 1879. (Courtesy of Little Traverse Region Historical Museum, Petoskey.)

Clifton House, a good vantage point for viewing the Fourth of July parade, 1890. (Courtesy of Little Traverse Region Historical Museum, Petoskey.)

Top: The Oriental Hotel, located at 210 East Lake Street. (Courtesy of Little Traverse Region Historical Museum, Petoskey.)

Left: The National Hotel, located at 316–318 East Lake Street, opened in 1883. (Courtesy of Little Traverse Region Historical Museum, Petoskey.)

Street Scenes

Petoskey's businesses responded to diverse patrons during the Hemingway years. The local residents needed provisions and supplies year-round and dry goods, hardware, grocery, and other stores met their needs. But increasingly businesses catered to the tourists. Mitchell and Lake streets developed as the main business section along with the Midway (an arcade area closer to the docks), supplying an increasing number of inexpensive tourist-targeted items such as Native American souvenirs and crafts, postcards of local scenes, and stones such as agates. As in any town, special events such as the Fourth of July were occasions for parades, and there is evidence that the Hemingways came to town to see these. Circuses also came, as did Pawnee Bill's Western show. Bay View developed its own summer series of events and was a regular stopping point for speakers on the camp-meeting circuit.

Top: Looking west from the top of Bay Street. (Courtesy of Little Traverse Region Historical Museum, Petoskey.)

Bottom: The Petoskey skyline from atop the steeple at St. Frances Church. (Courtesy of Little Traverse Region Historical Museum, Petoskey.)

The D. N. White Bakery, located on Mitchell
Street next to the current JC Penney store.
(Courtesy of Little Traverse Region Historical
Museum, Petoskey.)

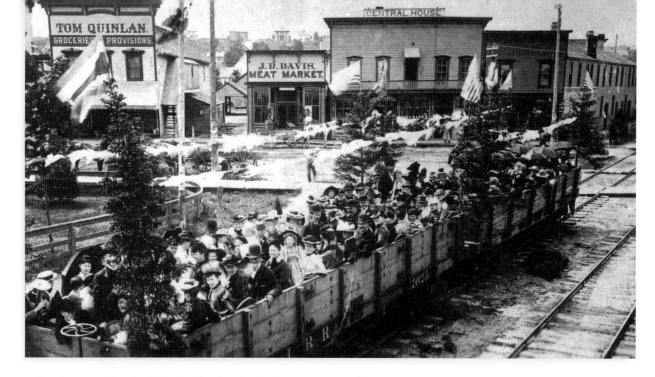

Top: A group of Fourth of July picnickers head to Bay View in an open rail car. (Courtesy of Little Traverse Region Historical Museum, Petoskey.)

Bottom: 401 Lake Street in the 1890s. Street advertisements announce vaudeville acts and the arrival of Pawnee Bill's Wild West show. (Courtesy of Little Traverse Region Historical Museum, Petoskey.)

Today's City Park Grill is pictured on the right butting up against the Cushman House Hotel. Although prohibition was in effect in Petoskey, it is likely Hemingway frequented this Lake Street establishment when he lived in Petoskey in 1919. (Courtesy of Little Traverse Region Historical Museum, Petoskey.)

Right: Mitchell Street parade. (Courtesy of Little Traverse Region Historical Museum, Petoskey.)

Bottom: The Midway. This collection of shops sold various tourist items including postcards and those associated with Native Americans. (Courtesy of Little Traverse Region Historical Museum, Petoskey.)

Clarence and Grace Hemingway in Petoskey, 1905. This was likely taken at a studio at the Midway. (Courtesy of the Ernest Hemingway Collection at the John F. Kennedy Presidential Library, Boston.)

Right and far right: Marcelline and Ernest Hemingway and friend in front of Fochtman's department store on Mitchell Street. (Courtesy of the Ernest Hemingway Collection at the John F. Kennedy Presidential Library, Boston.)

PLEASE CALL AT

McCarthy's Barber Shop and Bath Room

FOR A

First Class Hair Cut or Shave

A1 Workmen in Attendance

Corner Howard St.
and Park Avenue

C. H. McCarthy, Proprietor

Above: McCarthy's barbershop is thought to have inspired the one described in Hemingway's *Torrents of Spring.* (Courtesy of Little Traverse Region Historical Museum, Petoskey.)

He turned sharply around the corner of the barber shop and onto the Main Street of Petoskey. It was a handsome, broad street, lined on either side with brick and pressed stone buildings.

Torrents of Spring, 27.

Mitchell Street. (Courtesy of Little Traverse Region Historical Museum, Petoskey.)

Waterfront

At the turn of the twentieth century, the waterfront was not the recreational area it is today. It was a working area with the Pere Marquette railroad station and its busy rail lines, the City of Petoskey pier where the small and large steamships docked, and a place of souvenir stores, boat building companies, and fishermen's shanties. Two appendages jutted into Little Traverse Bay—the breakwater and pier. As its name implies, the breakwater provided a safe artificial harbor to protect boats docking at the pier. There was a constant flow of people coming and going from this area up through the Midway to the business section of town.

Left: The waterfront view as seen from the Bay View bluff. (Author's collection.)

Above: Petoskey from the harbor. Note the New Arlington Hotel on the far left edge. (Courtesy of Clarke Historical Library, Central Michigan University, Mount Pleasant.)

Below: View of businesses, the steamship pier, and construction of the breakwater. (Courtesy of Little Traverse Region Historical Museum, Petoskey.)

Steamers docked at the pier. (Courtesy of Little Traverse Region Historical Museum, Petoskey.)

Before the steamships used the piers, schooners did. (Courtesy of Little Traverse Region Historical Museum, Petoskey.)

Waterfront showing agate shops, fishermen's nets, and steamships. (Courtesy of Little
Traverse Region Historical Museum, Petoskey.)

The Petoskey Boat Company with the breakwater and pier in the background.
(Courtesy of Little Traverse Region Historical Museum, Petoskey.)

PERCH FISHING ON THE BREAKWATER, PETOSKEY, MICH.

Yogi walked on up the hill and turned to the left onto the Charlevoix road. He passed the last house of the outskirts of Petoskey and came out onto the open country road. On his right was a field that stretched to Little Traverse Bay. The blue of the bay opening out onto the big Lake Michigan. Across the bay the pine hills behind Harbor Springs. Beyond, where you could not see it, Cross Village where the Indians lived. Even further beyond, the Straits of Mackinac with St. Ignace, . . . [and] the Soo, both Canadian and American. There the wilder spirits of Petoskey sometimes went to drink beer. They were happy then.

Torrents of Spring, 52.

Fishing for perch on the breakwater in Petoskey. (Courtesy of Clarke Historical Library, Central Michigan University, Mount Pleasant.)

Another view of the Petoskey breakwater. (Courtesy of Little Traverse Region Historical Museum, Petoskey.)

Pere Marquette Railroad Depot

In 1892 the waterfront changed with the arrival of the new Chicago and West Michigan railroad depot. By 1900 it had become the Pere Marquette depot and was operating the "Resort Special," competing with the GR & I and offering Pullman car service from locations such as Detroit. Focusing on Charlevoix as much as Petoskey, the Pere Marquette also ran a dummy train system that featured an electric engine.

PERE MARQUETTE DEPOT AND PARK, PETOSKEY, MICHIGAN

The Pere Marquette station was located adjacent to the dock and breakwater. (Courtesy of Clarke Historical Library, Central Michigan University, Mount Pleasant.)

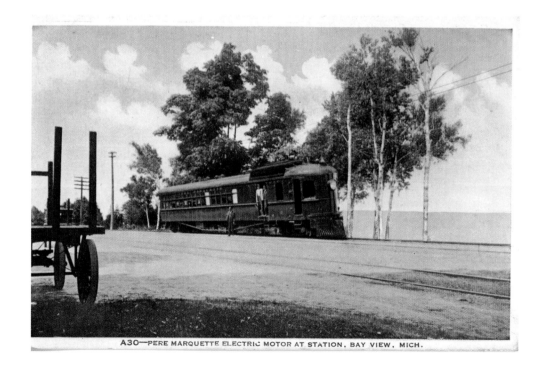

A30—PERE MARQUETTE ELECTRIC MOTOR AT STATION, BAY VIEW, MICH.

The electric trolley ran from the station to Bay View. (Courtesy of Little Traverse Region Historical Museum, Petoskey.)

A Chicago and West Michigan train in 1895 pulling a coach labeled "Charlevoix the Beautiful." (Courtesy of Little Traverse Region Historical Museum, Petoskey.)

The station was built in 1892 and is
currently a museum operated by the
Little Traverse Regional Historical Society.
(Courtesy of Little Traverse Region Historical
Museum, Petoskey.)

WALLOON LAKE AND VILLAGE

For the Hemingways, the last leg of the journey to their cottage involved boarding a suburban train in Petoskey bound for the village of Walloon. Located at the "foot" (southernmost part) of the lake, the village consisted of the rail station and a handful of businesses and lodgings. It was the principal boat dock for the small steamboats that served the lake resorts and cottages. The Hemingways (and others who spent time on Walloon Lake) had porters unload their luggage from the dummy train and then took one of the wood-burning steamships either to their own dock or to an established one nearby, from where their belongings would be taken to their cottage. Over the years several steamships served on this lake, including the *Tourist,* the *Rapid Transit,* and the *Outing.* The ships circled the lake daily, delivering people, mail, and provisions. It is said that the ships would stop at individual docks if signaled to do so.

Walloon village on Walloon Lake. (Courtesy of Clarke Historical Library, Central Michigan University, Mount Pleasant.)

Walloon rail station with a typical load of baggage. The Hemingways would have used this station on their travels to and from their cottage. (Courtesy of Little Traverse Region Historical Museum, Petoskey.)

Haynes Boat Livery at Walloon village. (Courtesy of Little Traverse Region Historical Museum, Petoskey.)

The New Walloon was located in Walloon village and was one of several resort hotels located on the lake. (Courtesy of Little Traverse Region Historical Museum, Petoskey.)

THE NEW WALLOON, WALLOON LAKE, MICH.

THE NEW WALLOON.

The Merrill Boat Livery with the *Outing* (*left*) and *Tourist* (*right*) moored. (Courtesy of Little Traverse Region Historical Museum, Petoskey.)

A group of young people socializing on the pier at the village. (Courtesy of Little Traverse Region Historical Museum, Petoskey.)

The steamers *Tourist* and *Outing*, Walloon Lake. (Courtesy of Clarke Historical Library, Central Michigan University, Mount Pleasant.)

The *Tourist* in dry dock. (Courtesy of Little Traverse Region Historical Museum, Petoskey.)

The *Tourist* with passengers. (Courtesy of Little Traverse Region Historical Museum, Petoskey.)

The *Outing* on Walloon Lake. (Courtesy of Little Traverse Region Historical Museum, Petoskey.)

The Echo Beach Inn was close to Bacon's Landing on Walloon Lake, and the Hemingways stayed there on at least one occasion. (Courtesy of Little Traverse Region Historical Museum, Petoskey.)

Clarence and Grace Hemingway with daughters Ursula, Madelaine, and Carol waiting for the steamship at Bacon's Landing on Walloon Lake. Ernie and Marcelline had gone ahead of the rest of the family, taking the SS *Manitou*. (Courtesy of Jim Sanford and Clarke Historical Library, Central Michigan University, Mount Pleasant.)

2

The Hemingway Family in Michigan

Clarence with his parents, Petoskey, 1914. (Courtesy of Jim Sanford and Clarke Historical Library, Central Michigan University, Mount Pleasant.)

The Family

Dr. Clarence Hemingway

Ernest's father, Clarence Edmonds "Ed" Hemingway, graduated from Oberlin College and Rush Medical College and practiced medicine in his hometown, Oak Park, Illinois. Working from his home office, he made house calls with his horse and cart before eventually switching over to a Model T Ford. His own father, Anson, was a successful Oak Park businessman who specialized in real estate and who passed on to Clarence the importance of raising children in a strict Christian household. Fascinated with science and the natural world, Clarence taught his children to be careful observers. He collected Native American artifacts, and in his home office he had snakes preserved in jars as well as medical and scientific books.

Dr. Hemingway, stricter with their children than his wife, was a keen believer that a good life was an active life. He disliked idleness, always encouraging his children to be doing "something." He introduced Ernest to the natural world and to fishing and hunting. Clarence's eyesight and shooting ability were outstanding, as was his cooking. To Dr. Hemingway, northern Michigan (and the

Clarence shooting clay pigeons at Windemere. He had a barrel of them shipped from Chicago and taught all his children—girls included—to shoot. (Courtesy of the Ernest Hemingway Collection at the John F. Kennedy Presidential Library, Boston.)

active lifestyle possible there) was an Eden. During the summers he joined his family at their cottage as often as his work would allow. Over the years, Dr. Hemingway suffered from ill health, a "nervous condition," and financial troubles and, as a result, his Michigan visits became less regular. In 1928, suffering from depression, diabetes, and angina, he committed suicide, an event that haunted Ernest for the rest of his life.

Nicholas Adams started thinking about his father. When he first thought about him it was always the eyes. The big frame, the quick movements, the wide shoulders, the hooked, hawk nose, the beard that covered the weak chin, you never thought about—it was always the eyes. . . . Nick could not write about him yet, although he would, later, but the quail country made him remember him as he was when Nick was a boy and he was very grateful to him for two things, fishing and shooting. His father was as sound on those two things as he was unsound on sex, for instance, and Nick was glad it had been that way; for someone has to give you your first gun or the opportunity to get it and use it, and you have to live where there is game or fish if you are to learn about them, and now, at thirty-eight, he loved to fish and to shoot exactly as much as when he first had gone with his father. It was a passion that had never slackened and he was very grateful to his father for bringing him to know it.

"Fathers and Sons," in *Nick Adams Stories*, 257.

Clarence and Ernest in 1917, the year Ernest graduated from high school. (Courtesy of the Ernest Hemingway Collection at the John F. Kennedy Presidential Library, Boston.)

Clarence with Ernest and Marcelline, 1901. (Courtesy of the Ernest Hemingway Collection at the John F. Kennedy Presidential Library, Boston.)

Clarence at Windemere in the 1920s with the rowboat *Ursula of Windemere* behind him. (Courtesy of the Ernest Hemingway Collection at the John F. Kennedy Presidential Library, Boston.)

Clarence cooking over an open fire at Longfield Farm. (Courtesy of the Ernest Hemingway Collection at the John F. Kennedy Presidential Library, Boston.)

Grace Hall Hemingway

Grace Hall was a strong-willed woman who saw her responsibility to her family as being artistic rather than domestic. Prior to her marriage to Clarence Hemingway in 1896, she had prepared for a life as a professional vocalist, but that ambition was never fully realized as she claimed stage lighting hurt her sensitive eyes. She was very active and well known in Oak Park and saw to it that all her children were trained as musicians—including Ernest, who grudgingly endured years playing the cello. She took them to the opera, concerts, and art galleries to refine their tastes. She was a very successful voice teacher whose earnings, some years, were said to exceed those of her doctor husband. For all the artistic skills she exhibited, she had very few domestic ones. She rarely cooked or did any housework; nurses, housekeepers, and cooks took care of the children and house for her—even in northern Michigan, where she either brought along an Oak Park helper or hired a local girl. In some ways, one could argue, her life at Windemere resembled hers at Oak Park. While a hired girl tended to housework, cooking, and caring for the children, Grace sang and read to her family, planned her children's activities (that she then recorded in each child's albums) and entertained guests from the area or faraway places.

Over time tensions grew between Ernest and his domineering mother—particularly during the summers, when he often was asked to assume Clarence's responsibilities during his father's frequent absences from Windemere. Ernest much preferred being with friends or fishing to splitting wood, burying trash, doing repairs, and dealing with his mother and four sisters. There was eventually an incident, in July 1920, that caused Grace to banish him from the cottage. While that rift was eventually settled, clearly these were two strong-willed people, and when she was critical of his early published writing, he distanced himself from her even more. Eventually his resentment hardened: he would claim that he hated her and he blamed her for his father's suicide. Despite this, family was family and while he communicated with her infrequently, he did set up a trust fund for her that would support her until her death in 1951. In return she gave him Windemere Cottage—hoping he would bring his own children there to spend summers the way he had.

Grace Hall shortly before her marriage, 1895. (Courtesy of Jim Sanford and Clarke Historical Library, Central Michigan University, Mount Pleasant.)

Left: Grace with Marcelline on the SS *State of Ohio* on the way to Michigan, 1898. (Courtesy of Jim Sanford and Clarke Historical Library, Central Michigan University, Mount Pleasant.)

Below: Grace with Ernest and Marcelline at Windemere, August 1900. (Courtesy of the Ernest Hemingway Collection at the John F. Kennedy Presidential Library, Boston.)

Family Members

Clarence and Grace Hemingway raised their six children in their own hometown of Oak Park. This nearest suburb located west of Chicago offered the benefits of small-town life combined with easy access to the city's culture and employment. Dr. Hemingway and Grace Hall, both from respected middle-class Oak Park families, were schoolmates who came to know each other well when Clarence treated Grace's mother during her final battle with cancer. They were married in 1896, months after her mother's death, and took up residence with Grace's widowed father, Ernest Hall, at his large Victorian home at 439 North Oak Park Avenue. The arrangement worked well and remained in place until his death in 1905. Grace desired a more stylish and impressive home so her father's was sold, and she used the profits from it and her inheritance to build a modern home on a double lot at 600 North Kenilworth Avenue. She designed the dwelling, which included a balconied two-story thirty-by-thirty-foot music room where she could give

Ernest, Ursula, Grace, and Marcelline on the Windemere beach. (Courtesy of the Ernest Hemingway Collection at the John F. Kennedy Presidential Library, Boston.)

Clarence and Grace Hall Hemingway at the time of their 1896 marriage. (Courtesy of the Ernest Hemingway Collection at the John F. Kennedy Presidential Library, Boston.)

lessons and hold recitals. The house also had a private entrance and space for Dr. Hemingway's medical practice. The Hemingway children (Marcelline, b. 1898; Ernest, b. 1899; Ursula, b. 1901; Madelaine "Sunny," b. 1904; Carol, b. 1911; and Leicester, b. 1915) took advantage of Oak Park's excellent schools, strong religious community, and cultural opportunities. While it was a great place to raise a family, the summer's heat and humidity could be stifling, making the clear air and cool northern Michigan nights a welcome change.

Grace's father, Ernest Hall's, home in Oak Park. Ernest Hemingway was born and lived here until 1906. It has been beautifully restored by the Oak Park Hemingway Foundation and now is now open to the public. (Courtesy of the Ernest Hemingway Collection at the John F. Kennedy Presidential Library, Boston.)

The Hemingway home at 600 North Kenilworth Avenue in Oak Park. Grace designed this home, where Ernest lived until 1919. (Courtesy of the Ernest Hemingway Collection at the John F. Kennedy Presidential Library, Boston.)

Top, left: Ernest (ten months), Grace, Clarence, and Marcelline (two years, four months), May 21, 1900. (Courtesy of Jim Sanford and Clarke Historical Library, Central Michigan University, Mount Pleasant.)

Top, right: The Hemingway family at Windemere on July 13, 1915. *Left to right:* Clarence, Carol, Marcelline, Madelaine, Grace with Leicester, Ernest, and Ursula. (Courtesy of Jim Sanford and Clarke Historical Library, Central Michigan University, Mount Pleasant.)

Left: Marcelline, Madelaine, Clarence, Grace, Ursula, and Ernest. (Courtesy of Jim Sanford and Clarke Historical Library, Central Michigan University, Mount Pleasant.)

WINDEMERE

In 1898 Clarence and Grace Hemingway traveled to northern Michigan (along with the infant Marcelline and her nurse), where they stayed at Bear Lake (later renamed Walloon Lake) with Grace's cousin. This beautiful spring-fed lake was deep, clear, and in the summer's light resembled the Caribbean blue water Ernest would enjoy later in life. Fish were plentiful (primarily bass and trout), and surrounding the lake were forests of maple, poplar, and cedar and some cleared farmland. It was a picture-perfect place to be. Unlike many families who preferred the leisure lifestyle available at resort hotels, the Hemingways decided to purchase property and build a simple cottage in which they planned to spend their summers. After rowing around the lake looking at available land, they purchased a large double lot from a local farmer, Henry Bacon, and headed back to Oak Park.

A year later, in September 1899, they returned, bringing their weeks-old son, Ernest, with them, to inspect their property and formally identify the site for the cottage they named Windemere.

Designed by Grace, Windemere cost $400 to build and was a simple, functional structure measuring twenty by forty feet. Facing southwest, it included a living room dominated by a large brick fireplace and two window seats that doubled as children's beds. Additionally, it had two small bedrooms and a kitchen complete with a wood-burning range and an iron-handled pump that supplied fresh well water. Oil lamps provided evening reading light and a piano, music for sing-alongs. White pine was used on both the interior and exterior, where the clapboards were painted white. The porch was a perfect place to look out at the lake and to watch the children play. While water for drinking came from the well, bathing and clothes washing was done with the cool lake water. An outhouse was discreetly tucked in a pine grove at the back of the property and a split-rail fence separated them from their farmer neighbors, the Bacons. The beach was sandy and the beautiful blue water got deeper gradually—perfect for swimming with young children. Birch, cedar, maple, and beech trees surrounded the lot, and tree-covered Murphy's Point protected the property from northern winds. Summer 1900 was the first one the family spent there and over the years, as the family grew, so did the cottage. A kitchen wing and screened-in porch were added, and later a separate three-bedroom sleeping annex was built behind the cottage for the children. A boathouse provided a safe place to store the canoe, rowboats and, eventually, the power launch.

At the time of his death in 1961, Ernest still owned Windemere, though he had not been there for decades. His widow (following a request he had made years earlier) signed over the property to his sister Sunny (Madelaine) and she used it as a seasonal home until her death. The cottage remains in the family and is not open to the public.

Dr. Hemingway on the SS *State of Ohio* on his way to Michigan for the first time in 1898. (Courtesy of Jim Sanford and Clarke Historical Library, Central Michigan University, Mount Pleasant.)

"Mama and Ernest sitting on the terrace of the future 'Windemere' / Walloon Lake cottage started the day Ernest was 8 weeks old and Marcelline, 20 months old, September 15, 1899" (Grace Hemingway, in Ernest's photo scrapbook). (Courtesy of the Ernest Hemingway Collection at the John F. Kennedy Presidential Library, Boston.)

On September 5, Tuesday, Ernest 6 1/2 weeks old went to Walloon Lake with Mama, Papa, and Nurse Norris on the steamship *Manitou*. September 6 had several pictures taken on our land in the Michigan woods on shore of lake.

Grace Hemingway, in Ernest's photo scrapbook, JFK.

Left: Photo of the Walloon Lake shoreline, taken by Clarence Hemingway in 1898. (Courtesy of Jim Sanford and Clarke Historical Library, Central Michigan University, Mount Pleasant.)

Below: Clarence Hemingway on Windemere beach, September 1899. (Courtesy of Jim Sanford and Clarke Historical Library, Central Michigan University, Mount Pleasant.)

Next page, top: Henry and Elizabeth Bacon sold the Hemingways the Walloon Lake property and became their neighbors and friends. (Courtesy of Jim Sanford and Clarke Historical Library, Central Michigan University, Mount Pleasant.)

Next page, bottom: Windemere during construction, 1899. (Courtesy of Jim Sanford and Clarke Historical Library, Central Michigan University, Mount Pleasant.)

Windemere before being painted and with shutters in place. (Courtesy of Jim Sanford and Clarke Historical Library, Central Michigan University, Mount Pleasant.)

The completed cottage, summer 1900. (Courtesy of the Ernest Hemingway Collection at the John F. Kennedy Presidential Library, Boston.)

Grace, Marcelline, Clarence, and Ernest in front of the cottage, 1901. (Courtesy of the Ernest Hemingway Collection at the John F. Kennedy Presidential Library, Boston.)

Kitchen wing addition, 1902. The family planted the trees in the foreground to provide shade. (Courtesy of Jim Sanford and Clarke Historical Library, Central Michigan University, Mount Pleasant.)

Cottage with Walloon Lake in the background. (Courtesy of the Ernest Hemingway Collection at the John F. Kennedy Presidential Library, Boston.)

The fireplace provided heat for the cottage, ca. 1900. (Courtesy of the Ernest Hemingway Collection at the John F. Kennedy Presidential Library, Boston.)

Grace was fond of playing music at Windemere and composed and published a song titled "Lovely Walloona." The door on the right goes out to the porch facing the lake, ca. 1900. (Courtesy of the Ernest Hemingway Collection at the John F. Kennedy Presidential Library, Boston.)

Originally the built-in seats on either side of the fireplace served as beds for Ernest and Marcelline, ca. 1900. The storage space under them was also useful. Note the number of prints on the walls. Even in northern Michigan, the family was surrounded with art. (Courtesy of the Ernest Hemingway Collection at the John F. Kennedy Presidential Library, Boston.)

Top: The door in the center and the one on the far right were to Windemere's two separate bedrooms, ca. 1900. (Courtesy of the Ernest Hemingway Collection at the John F. Kennedy Presidential Library, Boston.)

Bottom: Bedroom doors shown again. The door to the lake is on the far right. (Courtesy of Jim Sanford and Clarke Historical Library, Central Michigan University, Mount Pleasant.)

Top: The Hemingway property from an adjacent hill with boathouse visible but Windemere hidden in the trees. (Courtesy of Jim Sanford and Clarke Historical Library, Central Michigan University, Mount Pleasant.)

Bottom: Ernest, Grace, Clarence, and Marcelline on their beach, 1901. (Courtesy of Jim Sanford and Clarke Historical Library, Central Michigan University, Mount Pleasant.)

The back fencerow with the Bacon farm property to the left. Ernest would travel this route often, fetching the day's supply of milk in a mason jar. (Courtesy of Jim Sanford and Clarke Historical Library, Central Michigan University, Mount Pleasant.)

Nick walked barefoot along the path through the meadow below the barn. The path was smooth and the dew cool on his bare feet. He climbed a fence at the end of the meadow, went down through a ravine, his feet wet in the swamp mud, and then climbed up through the dry beech woods until he saw the lights of the cottage.

"Ten Indians," in *Nick Adams Stories*, 30.

Summers at the Cottage

The Hemingways' Michigan summers were in great contrast to Oak Park, where they lived in a bustling suburb filled with city sights and sounds. There there was school to attend, church, concerts, professional responsibilities, and obligations. All changed when they arrived at Windemere and a different, more relaxed routine took over. First, though, the cottage needed to be prepared: shutters removed, windows opened, floors swept, and trunks unloaded. Winter sticks and debris were removed from the yard, the hammock rehung, the dock put in, and the boats inspected. How different those first summer nights must have been from the days before. City sounds were replaced with the lapping of the water on the shore and the wind blowing through the trees. Nights were not spent tossing and turning in the city's heat and humidity but instead under the warmth of a favorite blanket as the cool night air chilled the cottage.

But the summers were not without responsibilities. Chores were assigned based on age and everyone contributed. Wood for the stove was split, stones removed from the yard, the beach raked, and garbage that could not be burned needed to be buried. Food was secured from a variety of sources. Staples such as flour, sugar, slab bacon, and chocolate were shipped from stores such as Montgomery Wards and fresh milk, cream, and meat often came from the Hemingways' neighbors, the Bacons. Vegetables were eventually grown on the Hemingways' own farm or purchased locally. Sometimes grocers in Walloon village or in Petoskey supplied favorites like popcorn and marshmallows.

Grace kept up her correspondence, especially when Clarence had to stay behind in Oak Park. The children were allowed to check out books from the Oak Park library for the summer, and they were read and reread along with the favorites left year-round at Windemere. There were also local friends to visit, like the Bacons and Dilworths and fellow summer resorters. And then there were familiar placed to see—Horton Bay and Creek, Petoskey, Charlevoix, Boyne City, the Black, Sturgeon, and Bear rivers. Once the family was settled into the summer routine, the season must have seemed so short for the children and so long for Grace, who over the years spent increasingly long periods of time at Windemere without Clarence and with increasing numbers of children. There was always a girl hired to do most of the household chores, but for someone like Grace, so connected to and involved with Oak Park's society, the summers must have become a challenge.

On and in the Water

As people who own or stay at lakeside cottages know, life there tends to revolve around the water. This was certainly true of the Hemingways. The lake served as a means of transportation and communication and as a source of food and recreation. Originally the family had a canoe, then a single rowboat named *Marcelline of Windemere*. A second boat (*Ursula of Windemere*) was added when they purchased property across the lake from Windmere in 1905, and in 1920 an eighteen-foot launch powered by a Gray Marine inboard engine named *Sunny* (in honor of Madelaine's nickname) found a home at the Hemingway's dock.

Dr. Hemingway with Marcelline, 1900. The washtub doubled as a boat and bath. (Courtesy of the Ernest Hemingway Collection at the John F. Kennedy Presidential Library, Boston.)

Walloon Lake, Mich.,

"Windemere"

"Ernest Miller went to Windemere, Walloon Lake, the day he was 11 months old. (June 21, 1900) He is perfectly fearless after the first time bathing in the lake—in fact [he] will creep out so far into the water that he has to be brought back. At 11 months had his picture taken in the water with his sister—'swimming like Papa' as he thinks" (Grace Hemingway, in Ernest's photo scrapbook). This image is one of several versions of picture postcards the family had made from original photographs and used to send summertime notes. (Courtesy of the Ernest Hemingway Collection at the John F. Kennedy Presidential Library, Boston)

Family photo in the *Ursula* (Carol, Ernest, Ursula, Marcelline, Madelaine, and Leicester), 1915. (Courtesy of Jim Sanford and Clarke Historical Library, Central Michigan University, Mount Pleasant.)

Right: Then as now, splashing your siblings was a popular activity. Ernest is in the back. (Courtesy of Jim Sanford and Clarke Historical Library, Central Michigan University, Mount Pleasant.)

Below: Clarence, Leicester, Ernest, Carol, Ursula, Marcelline, and Madelaine swimming at Windemere, 1915. (Courtesy of Jim Sanford and Clarke Historical Library, Central Michigan University, Mount Pleasant.)

Left: The Hemingway children posing on the shore, 1917. Left to right: Ursula, Madelaine, Marcelline, Ernest, Leicester, and Carol. (Courtesy of Jim Sanford and Clarke Historical Library, Central Michigan University, Mount Pleasant.)

Below: Ernest and sisters gathering netted minnows. (Courtesy of Jim Sanford and Clarke Historical Library, Central Michigan University, Mount Pleasant.)

Bacons' Farm

Immediately behind the Hemingway's property was the Bacon farm. The Bacons supplied the Hemingways with milk, cream, and other food items, and the children loved spending time there with them and their animals. In 1900 the Hemingways were invited to a barn raising, and Dr. Hemingway photographed the event. He was especially honored to be asked to drive in the final wooden spike. It was also on this June day, Grace recorded, that Ernest took his first steps. The Bacons were valued friends and provided inspiration for the fictional Garner family in Nick Adams stories such as "Ten Indians."

"Grandma and Grandpa Bacon" with grandson, Carl. (Courtesy of Jim Sanford and Clarke Historical Library, Central Michigan University, Mount Pleasant.)

Next page: The pathway to the Bacons' farm beyond the fencerow. (Courtesy of Jim Sanford and Clarke Historical Library, Central Michigan University, Mount Pleasant.)

They went down the hill and across the long field and through the orchard and then through a rail fence and into a field of stubble. Going through the stubble field they looked to the right and saw the slaughterhouse and the big barn in the hollow and the old log farmhouse on the other high land that overlooked the lake. The long road of Lombardy poplars that ran to the lake was in the moonlight.

"The Last Good Country," in *Nick Adams Stories*, 83.

"At 13 months driving sheep with a stick and shouting," 1900 (Grace Hemingway, in Ernest's photo scrapbook). (Courtesy of the Ernest Hemingway Collection at the John F. Kennedy Presidential Library, Boston.)

A barn raising on the Bacon farm, 1900. (Courtesy of the Ernest Hemingway Collection at the John F. Kennedy Presidential Library, Boston.)

There was a log house, chinked white with mortar, on a hill above the lake. There was a bell on a pole by the door to call people in to meals. Behind the house were fields and behind the fields was the timber. A line of Lombardy poplars ran from the house to the dock. Other poplars ran along the point. A road went up the hills along the edge of the timber and along that road he picked blackberries.

"The Snows of Kilimanjaro," in *Complete Short Stories*, 50.

The Bacons' log cabin homestead.
(Courtesy of Jim Sanford and Clarke Historical Library, Central Michigan University, Mount Pleasant.)

Diversions

Summers could get long for the Hemingways, as they typically stayed at Windemere from the time school got out until September. They created and participated in a number of activities to liven things up, such as costume parties and birthday trees. Since both Ernest and Carol celebrated their birthdays in July (Carol having been born at Windemere in 1911), the family cut and decorated an evergreen tree every July and placed it on the screened eating porch. And what would summer be without roasting marshmallows and camping out? The Hemingway children liked to camp on nearby Murphy's Point, where they had an old mattress and tent. It was just a quick run back to the security and comfort of Windemere if they became frightened or if the weather turned bad.

Top: Bringing back the birthday tree to celebrate Ernest's and Carol's July birthdays became a family tradition. Ernest is in the front, Grace sitting on the ground. (Courtesy of Jim Sanford and Clarke Historical Library, Central Michigan University, Mount Pleasant.)

Right: The children playing dress up, with Ernest wrapped in a bearskin. (Courtesy of Jim Sanford and Clarke Historical Library, Central Michigan University, Mount Pleasant.)

Carol Hemingway in a tent (*left*) and Madelaine "Sunny" Hemingway (*bottom left*) making faces for the camera while camping at Murphy's Point on Walloon Lake. (Courtesy of Jim Sanford and Clarke Historical Library, Central Michigan University, Mount Pleasant.)

Roasting marshmallows—a tradition then and now. *Left to right:* Ursula, Marcelline, Ernest, and Madeleine. (Courtesy of the Ernest Hemingway Collection at the John F. Kennedy Presidential Library, Boston.)

Walloon Lake, Mich.

"*Windemere*"

Another Windemere postcard shows Ernest, Marcelline, and Ursula with Dr. Hemingway's coronet. It is said that he used this instrument to signal the Walloon Lake steamers to stop at his dock. (Courtesy of Jim Sanford and Clarke Historical Library, Central Michigan University, Mount Pleasant.)

"Windemere"

Walloon Lake, Michigan

Friday Morning Aug. 13. 1915

Dearest Marcelline

This letter arrived from Arabel this morning, so I opened it to see what her plans were, and hasten to send it on to you. I fear you will not meet — but it can't be helped.

Daddy took the three little girls down on the "Rapid Transit" from our dock to see Nettie & Margarette off. They were very grateful for their good time. I'm sure it did Nettie a world of good. Be sure you express your gratitude for each and every kindness of the Ehrman friends. Daddy will write you about the trains, returning. It seems they have a new schedule beginning next Monday taking off some trains. They are making several changes in our little dollie road to Walloon, also.

Take good care of my girlie, ever so much love
from Mother
Gracie

Letters often traveled to and from Windemere. This one was sent to Marcelline from her mother, Grace. (Courtesy of Jim Sanford and Clarke Historical Library, Central Michigan University, Mount Pleasant.)

Guests

Both family and friends visited Windemere. Grace's uncle, Tyler Hancock, who regularly stayed with the family in Oak Park, also came to northern Michigan. He and Dr. Hemingway liked traveling to Michigan's Upper Peninsula, where they fished at Brevort Lake. According to Marcelline, one time they agreed to bring Ernest with them if he could learn his multiplication tables. With her help he did, and it is assumed he made his first trip to the Upper Peninsula that summer. Clarence's parents, Anson and Adelaide, made the long trip to Windemere, as did Grace's father. In 1911 a Hemingway family reunion was held, and twenty-two cousins swam while the grown-ups listened to stories told by Clarence's parents and brothers. There is little doubt that Ernest found those of his Uncle Willoughby, who was on a break from his work as missionary surgeon in China, the most interesting. Special occasions like the Fourth of July were marked by boats full of guests coming from as far away as Boyne City to enjoy pit-barbequed lamb, oven-roasted pig, potato salad, and gallons of lemonade. The highlight of the evening was when Dr. Hemingway fired off skyrockets and the children were allowed Roman candles and pinwheels nailed to the dock. Other regular visitors included neighbors and Native Americans who lived in the area.

Clarence and Grace's "Uncle Tyley" Hancock show off their catch. (Courtesy of Jim Sanford and Clarke Historical Library, Central Michigan University, Mount Pleasant.)

On his first birthday (July 21, 1900) he walked across the room. For company we invited about 90 guests on the lake to a housewarming of Windemere. There were 55 present. A perfect day. Tables were set out under the trees where lemonade and cake were served. A heaping washtub of popcorn looked very charming on the porch as the tub was trimmed in green crushed paper. Mama sang a number of songs to Miss Christine's accompaniment. Thirteen boats were drawn up on our shore looking quite Venetian. Ernest was very happy and played with all the children.

Grace Hemingway, in Ernest's photo scrapbook, JFK.

According to Grace, this photo was taken on Ernest's first birthday after the party guests had left, July 21, 1900. (Courtesy of Jim Sanford and Clarke Historical Library, Central Michigan University, Mount Pleasant.)

Top: Anson and Adelaide Hemingway at Windemere. (Courtesy of Jim Sanford and Clarke Historical Library, Central Michigan University, Mount Pleasant.)

Right: Clarence with his parents in Petoskey, 1914. (Courtesy of Jim Sanford and Clarke Historical Library, Central Michigan University, Mount Pleasant.)

Top: Guests at Ernest's fifteenth birthday party, July 21, 1914. Grace sits smiling at the head of the table. (Courtesy of Jim Sanford and Clarke Historical Library, Central Michigan University, Mount Pleasant.)

Left: Grace labeled this photo "Mrs. Nick Bolton and her children, Ottawa Indians." It is possible that one of the girls in the picture was Prudence Bolton, a Native girl who inspired characters in the Nick Adams stories. (Courtesy of Jim Sanford and Clarke Historical Library, Central Michigan University, Mount Pleasant.)

Longfield Farm

In 1905 a forty-acre farm across the lake from Windemere was being sold for back taxes, and Grace used part of her father's inheritance to buy it. Dr. Hemingway liked the potential for teaching his family the value of good, honest physical labor and for securing a food source during the summer months. Thus Longfield Farm was introduced into the family's summer routine. The Hemingways put in long hours planting trees—apple, black walnut, cherry, plum, peach, and evergreens—and vegetables. In good years there was enough surplus produce for the children to go around the lake selling potatoes, beets, carrots, and peas to other cottage owners and small resorts. Eventually Ernest would oversee the shipping of produce back to Oak Park, where it was enjoyed by the family year-round. Although he likely preferred to spend time fishing with friends to hours planting and digging potatoes, Ernest accepted his father's expectations. According to Ernest's brother, Leicester, Dr. Hemingway contracted work with Ernest and this provided Ernest with spending money while accomplishing the tasks Dr. Hemingway wanted done. By 1917 twenty additional acres were purchased and Warren Sumner, a local farmer, was hired as a tenant farmer. Ernest often slept at the farm in his tent and worked that summer with Sumner removing the old farmhouse, cutting twenty acres of hay, and building an icehouse that they then filled with sawdust. During the cold winter, Sumner stocked it with ice cut and hauled from Walloon Lake. All summer long, chunks of that ice were brought across the lake to Windemere and kept in an icebox under the trees until needed to preserve food or cool drinks on hot, muggy summer days. Eventually, staying at Longfield appealed to Ernest not only because it removed him from daily Windemere chores, but because it also put him closer to fishing and friends at Horton Bay. In 1919 Grace had a cottage built for herself on a high point of the property, much to her son and husband's dismay. "Grace Cottage" was a refuge for her, a place to which she could escape from hectic family life to a simple shelter equipped with her piano.

Clarence Hemingway preparing a chicken dinner at Longfield Farm. (Courtesy of the Ernest Hemingway Collection at the John F. Kennedy Presidential Library, Boston.)

Above: The view across Walloon Lake from the farm. Windemere was located straight across the lake from it. (Courtesy of the Ernest Hemingway Collection at the John F. Kennedy Presidential Library, Boston.)

Right: Clarence Hemingway cutting hay at Longfield. (Courtesy of Jim Sanford and Clarke Historical Library, Central Michigan University, Mount Pleasant.)

The potato crop placed in crates and then bagged. In the first photo (*left*), Madelaine is holding the reins of Warren Sumner's team of mules and Carol is posing in her dress. In the second (*below*), Warren and team haul the bagged potatoes, 1915. (Courtesy of Jim Sanford and Clarke Historical Library, Central Michigan University, Mount Pleasant.)

I came here [Pinehurst] last night from Walloon to get the mail and some more clothes. There will be about 60 bushels of marketable potatoes the way it looks now. Those 60 bu. however will be very good. . . . I dig them, then pick up the good ones and put them in crates and then sack them. . . . Today on the Missouri go down to you the barrel of apples I spoke about on the card. And I thought you could use a sack of spuds. The sack shows the general run of the good ones. Please write your instructions right away so if you want them shipped down I will send them next Wed. on the boat.

Letter to Clarence Hemingway, September 19, 1917, in *Selected Letters*, 1.

Left: Ernest atop a load of hay with Warren Sumner, 1917. (Courtesy of Jim Sanford and Clarke Historical Library, Central Michigan University, Mount Pleasant.)

Below: Longfield Farm on the west side of Walloon Lake showing the vegetable section, ca. 1915. (Courtesy of Jim Sanford and Clarke Historical Library, Central Michigan University, Mount Pleasant.)

Grace Cottage, built at Longfield Farm in 1919 as a getaway for Grace Hemingway.
(Courtesy of the Ernest Hemingway Collection at the John F. Kennedy Presidential Library, Boston.)

Warren Sumner and Ernest removing stones at Longfield, 1917 (Courtesy of Jim Sanford and Clarke Historical Library, Central Michigan University, Mount Pleasant.)

Went over to Longfield yesterday. Warren [Sumner] not there to speak to but talked to his wife. She said she had a letter from Mrs. Hemingway written Thursday engaging Warren to have the lumber for the house she was going to build. She said Warren was hurrying through his work so as to be ready to do the hauling. Don't know whether you know about this or not. Is mother going to this selfish piece of damn foolishness? The Dilworths asked me about it when I first came up and I told them "no" knowing your ultimatum. They said they couldn't understand why she would want to build there.

Letter to Clarence Hemingway, June 9, 1919, CMU.

All the cherry trees are loaded. . . . Practically all of the trees in the old orchard will bear fruit. All the Northern Spies and the early harvest apples too. In the old clover field back of the old orchard there will be quite a few apples in the young trees. The trees all look *good*. But need spraying if the fruit is to be salable. I asked Mrs. Sumner if Warren was going to spray trees and she said he had heard nothing from you. So I told her to tell him to go ahead and spray. You ought to have a big fruit crop. . . . Give my love to mother and tell her I'll write her.

Letter to Clarence Hemingway, June 9, 1919, CMU.

Road Trip from Oak Park

A typical road of the time in the Petoskey area, ca. 1915. (Courtesy of Little Traverse Region Historical Museum, Petoskey.)

The year 1917 saw a change in the way the Hemingways traveled to Michigan; for the first time Dr. Hemingway came in his Model T touring car. Ernest, Grace, and young Leicester accompanied him while the girls went ahead on the familiar steamship, SS *Manitou,* and met the family at Walloon. Dr. Hemingway's journal and family photos tell the story of the five-day journey, with nights in tents, freshly caught fish fried for breakfast, terrible roads, and adventure. The 487-mile trip had 100 miles added on for detours, and the family carried a shovel to use when the car became stuck on rutted roads. A 31-mile stretch between Traverse City and Walloon Lake was especially difficult. The road was only a sand track on which they averaged a whopping 8 miles an hour!

Later that summer, daughter Marcelline remembered Clarence driving to Petoskey over sand hills on unimproved roads. He carried a shovel and an ax to cut branches along the way. One can image his embarrassment when he became so stuck he needed to be pulled out by a laughing farmer and his team of horses. The return to Oak Park was much easier—the Hemingways and their car returned via steamship.

Clarence, Leicester, and Ernest (who wears his Oak Park High School letter sweater he earned as a member of the football team), 1917. (Courtesy of Jim Sanford and Clarke Historical Library, Central Michigan University, Mount Pleasant.)

Photo taken by Ernest of his parents and brother, Leicester, 1917. The car was the same one Clarence used on his medical rounds in Oak Park. (Courtesy of Jim Sanford and Clarke Historical Library, Central Michigan University, Mount Pleasant.)

A brief stop along the way. *Left to right:*
Grace, Leicester, and Ernest. (Courtesy of
Jim Sanford and Clarke Historical Library, Central
Michigan University, Mount Pleasant.)

The Hemingways pose with relatives at Benzonia,
Michigan, 1917. Clarence, Grace, and Leicester stand
in the center, with Ernest to the right of them. (Courtesy
of Jim Sanford and Clarke Historical Library, Central Michigan
University, Mount Pleasant.)

3

Ernest's Michigan: Fact and Fiction

Clarence Hemingway taught Ernest to love the out-of-doors and fishing. Ernest is touching Clarence's string of fish as Marcelline looks on, 1901. (Courtesy of Jim Sanford and Clarke Historical Library, Central Michigan University, Mount Pleasant.)

ERNEST AND MICHIGAN

Long before he was a famous author and personality, "Ernie" Hemingway was one of thousands of young people who came to stay in northern Michigan. He first visited as a six-week-old baby in 1899 when his family made final arrangements for Windemere's construction. His last documented visit was in 1947 when he stopped for a day en route to Wyoming. His Michigan time was filled with those leisure activities typically associated with summer—fishing, hiking, camping, enjoying the lakes and streams, and spending time with new and old friends. By the time he was in his teens he more often enjoyed the company of friends rather than family. At first these were schoolmates, like Harold Sampson or Lewis Clarahan, who joined him at the lake from Oak Park, but eventually they were replaced with other summer people like Bill and Katy Smith and his friends from the First World War. His sleeping quarters evolved from shared space with his sisters to a tent pitched behind the cottage and later, one across the lake at Longfield Farm.

While Hemingway did little writing in Michigan (other than correspondence) until the fall of 1919, he did take in and store for later use the places and people he experienced. It wasn't until he moved to Paris in the 1920s that his Michigan experiences began to turn into stories. Writing in cafés and in his room (where, it was reported, he had a Michigan map tacked up on the wall), he blended the real and imagined to create a character named Nick Adams and stories that seem so real that it is hard to believe they are fiction. But they are.

Ernest afloat in Walloon Lake, 1901. (Courtesy of Jim Sanford and Clarke Historical Library, Central Michigan University, Mount Pleasant.)

Ernest behind Windemere with his cap gun, ca. 1905. (Courtesy of Jim Sanford and Clarke Historical Library, Central Michigan University, Mount Pleasant.)

Ernest canoeing. (Courtesy of the Ernest Hemingway Collection at the John F. Kennedy Presidential Library, Boston.)

Ernest, likely writing a letter.
(Courtesy of the Ernest Hemingway
Collection at the John F. Kennedy
Presidential Library, Boston.)

Left: Ernest at age sixteen. (Courtesy of
the Ernest Hemingway Collection at the John F.
Kennedy Presidential Library, Boston.)

Above: Ernest and his friend Harold Sampson killed this porcupine, which had injured one of the Bacon family dogs, 1914. Dr. Hemingway's rule was that nothing was to be killed unless it was to be eaten, and this was the case with the porcupine (which Sampson remembered tasted like leather). (Courtesy of Jim Sanford and Clarke Historical Library, Central Michigan University, Mount Pleasant.)

Right: Ernest, proud of his catch. (Courtesy of the Ernest Hemingway Collection at the John F. Kennedy Presidential Library, Boston.)

Ernest eventually preferred sleeping in a tent behind
Windemere to sharing space with his four sisters. He's
shown here with a woodchuck he shot, ca. 1916. (Courtesy
of Jim Sanford and Clarke Historical Library, Central Michigan
University, Mount Pleasant.)

It was a pleasant café, warm and clean and friendly, and I hung up my old waterproof on the coat rack to dry and put my worn and weathered felt hat on the rack above the bench and ordered a *cafe au lait*. The waiter brought it and I took out a notebook from the pocket of the coat and a pencil and started to write. I was writing about up in Michigan and since it was a wild, cold, blowing day it was that sort of day in the story. I had already seen the end of fall come through boyhood, youth and young manhood, and in one place you could write about it better than in another. That was called transplanting yourself, I thought, and it could be as necessary with people as with other sorts of growing things.

"A Good Café on the Place St.-Michel," in *A Moveable Feast*, 5.

The only writing that was any good was what you made up, what you imagined. That made everything come true. . . . Everything good he had ever written he'd made up. None of it had ever happened. Other things had happened. Better things, maybe. That was what the family couldn't understand. They thought it was all experience. . . . Nick in the stories was never himself. He made him up. Of course he had never seen an Indian woman having a baby. That was what made it good. Nobody knew that.

"On Writing," in *Nick Adams Stories*, 237.

FISHING THE STREAMS AND LAKES

Fishing was a lifelong passion for Ernest Hemingway. While his pursuit of marlin and other saltwater game fish is well known, his love of stream and lake fishing was born in northern Michigan. Allegedly his first fishing outing was at age three, and his fourth birthday present was a day out fishing with his father. Despite the all-day rain, his mother claimed, he enjoyed the experience. Over the years he fished in Walloon Lake and Lake Charlevoix but seemed to have a special love of the small streams that produced brook and rainbow trout. He perhaps fished Horton Creek more than any other stream but also had great experiences on the Black and Sturgeon rivers near Vanderbilt and Wolverine, Michigan.

Ernest fishing in front of Windemere, 1901. (Courtesy of the Ernest Hemingway Collection at the John F. Kennedy Presidential Library, Boston.)

Both pages: Both of these images show Ernest on Horton Creek as a five-year-old. The one of him alone is well known but the other, showing him with Wesley Dilworth, is of interest as it reveals how many Michigan streams looked after the lumber era— choked with cuttings and slashings. (First courtesy of Jim Sanford and Clarke Historical Library, Central Michigan University, Mount Pleasant; second courtesy of the Ernest Hemingway Collection at the John F. Kennedy Presidential Library, Boston.)

Ernest with his catch, 1916. (Courtesy of Jim Sanford and Clarke Historical Library, Central Michigan University, Mount Pleasant.)

"Ernest Hemingway 14 years old. Four trout. His catch weighing 2lbs" (Grace Hemingway, in Marcelline Hemingway Sanford's photo scrapbook). (Courtesy of Jim Sanford and Clarke Historical Library, Central Michigan University, Mount Pleasant.)

And let me tell you about the rainbow fishing. I don't know whether you are a fisher man or not. But you might be a rank hater of the sport and you would like this kind of fishing. . . . A reel goes screeeeeeech, the tip of the rod jerks under water, you run down and grab it up and thumb the reel and then out in the lake a big rainbow shoots up into the air. And then the fight. And Jim those trout can fight. And I've never taken one under three pounds out of the [Horton] Bay and they run as high as fifteen. The biggest I ever took was nine and seven ounces. And you always get a strike. A night's fishing would average three of the big trout though I have taken as high as seven. It is the best rainbow trout fishing in America. Just this one bay and the only thing you can take them on is skinned perch. And nobody knows about it but us. People come down and troll all day for them from Charlevoix and never get a strike while we will be taking them all day.

Letter to Jim Gamble, April 27, 1919, CMU.

"Ernie's trout caught at Horton's Creek," 1916 (Grace Hemingway, in Marcelline Hemingway Sanford's photo scrapbook). (Courtesy of Jim Sanford and Clarke Historical Library, Central Michigan University, Mount Pleasant.)

Above: "Ernest camped all night at Horton's Creek and caught this fish," 1916 (Grace Hemingway, in Marcelline Hemingway Sanford's photo scrapbook). (Courtesy of Jim Sanford and Clarke Historical Library, Central Michigan University, Mount Pleasant.)

Right: The fisherman's pride is evident. Ernest, ca. 1916. (Courtesy of the Ernest Hemingway Collection at the John F. Kennedy Presidential Library, Boston.)

Ernest at Horton Bay with trout caught there, 1919 or 1920.
(Courtesy of the Ernest Hemingway Collection at the John F. Kennedy
Presidential Library, Boston.)

HIKING IN MICHIGAN

In 1915 and 1916 Ernest and his Oak Park friend Lewis Clarahan took extended hikes in northern Michigan. Hiking was a popular physical fitness fad in Oak Park, and the local YMCA had even hired a "hike master" in 1913 to coordinate excursions. Ernest and his friends had gone on several local hikes, including one in April 1915 to Lake Zurich, thirty-five miles from Oak Park. Later that spring, Ernest and Lewis planned a greater test of their endurance. On June 19 (the day school ended) they (along with friend Ray Ohlsen) boarded the steamship *Missouri* in Chicago and took it to Frankfort, Michigan. The boys must have been excited, and it was reported that the purser had to quiet them down in their stateroom. In Frankfort, Ray turned back for home while Ernest and Lewis began their five-day, hundred-mile journey on foot. Eating freshly caught trout and canned beans, they hiked and fished their way to

Walloon Lake by way of Traverse City, Elk Rapids, and Charlevoix. In 1916 they replicated the trip, taking the *Missouri* to Onekama. They then worked their way to Kalkaska via Bear Creek and the Boardman and Rapid rivers. At Kalkaska, Clarahan caught a Chicago-bound train and Ernest boarded one for Petoskey. After a night's stay at the Hotel Perry (where his room cost 75¢), he went to Horton Bay, where he enjoyed the hospitality of the Dilworth family until his own family arrived at Windemere.

Above: Ernest and Lewis Clarahan on a hike to Lake Zurich, Illinois, in the spring of 1915. (Courtesy of the Ernest Hemingway Collection at the John F. Kennedy Presidential Library, Boston.)

Left: The hikers took the SS *Missouri* to Michigan in 1915 and 1916. (Courtesy of Clarke Historical Library, Central Michigan University, Mount Pleasant.)

Left: Ernest and Lewis with their camping and fishing gear. (Courtesy of the Ernest Hemingway Collection at the John F. Kennedy Presidential Library, Boston.)

Above: Ernest relaxing at one of the 1916 hike campsites. (Courtesy of the Ernest Hemingway Collection at the John F. Kennedy Presidential Library, Boston.)

It's interesting to note that the journal he kept of the June 10–21, 1916, trip included the supplies he took, a record of the fish he and Clarahan caught, and a page listing "Good Stuff for Essays—Old Couple on Boardman [River], Mancelona-Indian girl, Bear Creek, Rapid River, Mancelona during night, tough talking lumberjack, young Indian girl kills self and girl." Locations and experiences from these trips show up in the short stories "The Battler" and "Light of the World."

I had different ways of occupying myself while I lay awake. I would think of a trout steam I had fished along when I was a boy and fish its whole length very carefully in my mind, fishing it very carefully under all the logs, all the turns of the bank, the deep holes and the clear shallow stretches, sometimes catching trout and sometimes losing them. I would stop fishing at noon to eat my lunch, sometimes on a log over stream, sometimes on a high bank under a tree, and I always ate my lunch very slowly and watched the stream below me while I ate.

"Now I Lay Me," in *Nick Adams Stories,* 144.

Ernest enjoyed fishing on the Boardman and Rapid rivers, Bear Creek, and in ponds created by dams. (Courtesy of the Ernest Hemingway Collection at the John F. Kennedy Presidential Library, Boston.)

Ernest arriving at Walloon Lake, his hiking and camping supplies on his back, 1916. (Courtesy of the Ernest Hemingway Collection at the John F. Kennedy Presidential Library, Boston.)

The blue backed notebooks, the two pencils, and the pencil sharpener (a pocket knife was too wasteful), the marble-topped tables, the smell of early morning, sweeping out and mopping, and luck were all you needed. For luck you carried a horse chestnut and a rabbit's foot in your right pocket. . . . Some days it went so well that you could make the country so that you could walk into it through the timber to come out into the clearing and work up on to the high ground and see the hills beyond the arm of the lake. A pencil lead might break off in the conical nose of the pencil sharpener and you would use the small blade of the pen knife to clear it or else sharpen the pencil carefully with the sharp blade and then slip your arm through the sweat-salted leather of your pack strap to lift the pack again, get the other arm through and feel the weight settle on your back and feel the pine needles under your moccasins as you started down for the lake.

"Birth of a New School," in *A Moveable Feast*, 91.

Horton Bay

In many ways the town of Horton Bay (located on Lake Charlevoix's Horton Bay) was the most important Michigan locale for Ernest Hemingway. Located about six miles from Windemere, it had been associated with lumbering, but by Ernest's time it had evolved into a quiet summer resort enclave. Between 1917 and his 1921 wedding, it was where he spent most of his Michigan time, visiting with summer friends, eating meals, and often fishing on Horton Creek or Horton Bay. At its heart was Pinehurst Cottage, an establishment run by Hemingway family friends Jim and Elizabeth Dilworth. Its chicken dinners were well known regionally, and diners came from distances to enjoy them. The Dilworths also rented rooms and often allowed Ernest to stay free on a back porch. Jim was the village blacksmith, and his shop was a popular gathering spot. Just outside the village was the Charles farm, where Bill and Katy Smith spent summers with their aunt, Mrs. Charles. Since their mother's death in 1899, she had raised the two and had bought and fixed up a farmhouse to provide healthy summers for them. The Smiths were from St. Louis, older than Ernest (Bill by four years, Katy by eight), and good company. Bill, an easy-to-get-along-with, slow-talking Missourian with a dry sense of humor and love of nicknames, fished with Hemingway and worked on the Charles's farm and the Hemingways' Longfield farm with him. Quick-witted Katy was a Hemingway favorite. Her green eyes and combined sisterly/motherly attention to him were welcomed. The Smiths and other summer people (including Carl Edgar, a Kansas City bachelor nicknamed "Odgar" who fawned over Katy) would often gather to talk or swim. Years later in Paris, Hemingway would write about this village and use the people he had known there as inspiration for fictional characters. The reader will find Horton Bay in "Up in Michigan," "The End of Something," "Three Day Blow," "Last Good Country," and "Summer People."

Today Horton Bay remains much the same as it was during Hemingway's time there. While the church in which he was married and the blacksmith shop are gone, the Red Fox Inn and general store are still active businesses open to the public. The Dilworths' Pinehurst Cottage and its annex, Shangri-La, are privately owned but retain their original appearance. Boaters and swimmers still enjoy the bay's cool waters, and the pilings for the warehouses and the dock Ernie and friends swam from are clearly visible.

Lumber mill workers stand in front of Stroud's Mill #2, located on Horton Bay close to today's Lake Street. Notice the barrel of water on the roof in case of fire. This mill was closed by the time Ernest arrived at Horton Bay, but tales of it were common. (Courtesy of Clarke Historical Library, Central Michigan University, Mount Pleasant.)

In the old days Hortons Bay [*sic*] was a lumbering town. No one who lived in it was out of sound of the big saws in the mill by the lake. Then one year there were no more logs in the mill by the lake. Lumber schooners came into the bay and were loaded with the cut of the mill that stood stacked in the yard. All the piles of lumber were carried away. The big mill building had all its machinery that was removable taken out and hoisted on board one of the schooners by the men who had worked in the mill. The schooner moved out of the bay toward the open lake, carrying two great saws, the traveling carriage that hurled the logs against the revolving circular saws and all the rollers, wheels, belts, and iron piled on a hull-deep load of lumber. Its open hold covered with canvas and lashed tight, the sails of the schooner filled and it moved out into the open lake, carrying with it everything that had made the mill a mill and Hortons Bay [*sic*] a town.

"The End of Something," in *Nick Adams Stories*, 200.

Hortons Bay [*sic*], the town, was only five houses on the main road between Boyne City and Charlevoix. There was the general store and post office with a high false front and maybe a wagon hitched out front, Smith's house, Stroud's house, Dillworth's house, Horton's house, and Van Hoosen's house. The houses were in a big grove of elm trees and the road was very sandy. There was farming country and timber each way up the road. Up the road a ways was the Methodist church and down the road the other direction was the township school. The blacksmith shop was painted red and faced the school.

"Up in Michigan," in *Complete Short Stories*, 59.

The Horton Bay General Store with the Red Fox Inn to the right. The store remains open and is a popular stop for those following Hemingway's Michigan footsteps. (Courtesy of Clarke Historical Library, Central Michigan University, Mount Pleasant.)

The Red Fox Inn began as a rooming house for area workers. Today it houses a Hemingway-focused bookstore run by Jim Hartwell, grandson of Vollie Fox, a friend of Ernest. (Courtesy of Clarke Historical Library, Central Michigan University, Mount Pleasant.)

Alanzo Stroud's house reflected his position as a mill and property owner. (Courtesy of Clarke Historical Library, Central Michigan University, Mount Pleasant.)

Jim Dilworth's blacksmith shop was a popular village gathering spot. (Courtesy of Clarke Historical Library, Central Michigan University, Mount Pleasant.)

The view toward Horton Bay on Lake Charlevoix with the Dilworths' Pinehurst Cottage in the foreground and Horton Bay Point in the background. (Courtesy of Jim Sanford and Clarke Historical Library, Central Michigan University, Mount Pleasant.)

A steep sandy road ran down the hill to the bay through the timber. From Smith's back door you could look out across the woods that ran down to the lake and across the bay. It was very beautiful in the spring and summer, the blue bay and bright and usually whitecaps on the lake out beyond the point from the breeze blowing from Charlevoix and Lake Michigan. From Smith's back door Liz could see ore barges way out in the lake going toward Boyne City.

"Up in Michigan," in *Complete Short Stories*, 60.

Across the [B]ay from where we would live is a point. And a little trout river comes into the Bay and makes a channel past this point. There is an old quay alongside and it is from there that we fish. And this is the manner of fishing. We paddle over across the bay and stop at this old lumber dock. Just level with the water. And from the dock we run out about four or five lines into the channel. These are baited with a whole skinned perch which is dropped into the channel and sinks to the bottom. The lines are run out and then we put a weight on the butt of the rod they are run out from and set the click on the reel and wait. Do you get the scene? All the rods sticking out over the side, the clicks set, and the lines running way out into the channel. Then if it is night we have a campfire on the point and sit around and yarn and smoke or if it is daytime we loaf around and read and await results.

Letter to Jim Gamble, April 27, 1919, CMU.

Above left: Lake Charlevoix's Horton Bay with the point in the background. Horton Creek empties into the bay to the right of this image. (Courtesy of the Ernest Hemingway Collection at the John F. Kennedy Presidential Library, Boston.)

Left: View across the bay from the point, a place where Hemingway enjoyed camping and picnicking. The village dock and warehouse buildings are visible at the right edge of this photo. (Courtesy of Little Traverse Region Historical Museum, Petoskey.)

Horton Creek was a favorite fishing stream of Hemingway's.
(Courtesy of Clarke Historical Library, Central Michigan University,
Mount Pleasant.)

The Bean and Potato houses were warehouses where farm
produce was stored awaiting the steamships that would
pick it up and carry it to market. They loaded from a wide
U-shaped dock that was also a popular gathering spot. At
times the large warehouse space was used for community
events such as dances. (Courtesy of Clarke Historical Library,
Central Michigan University, Mount Pleasant.)

Down the road through the trees he could see the white of the Bean
House on its piles over the water. . . . He walked down the road, past
the car and the big warehouse on the left where apples and potatoes
were loaded onto the boats in the fall, past the white-painted Bean
house where they danced by lantern light sometimes on the hardwood
floor, out on the dock to where they were swimming.

"Summer People," in *Nick Adams Stories*, 217.

Pinehurst employed local girls as waitresses in the summer. Shown here swimming in Horton Bay are some of them. *Left to right:* Helen Sly, Marjorie Bump, Connie Curtis, and Georgianna Bump. (Courtesy of Clarke Historical Library, Central Michigan University, Mount Pleasant.)

The SS *Missouri* stopped at the Horton Bay dock to deliver and pick up mail and freight. The deep channel through Charlevoix allowed the ship to dock at the inland lake—as shown here—before heading out to Lake Michigan. (Courtesy of Clarke Historical Library, Central Michigan University, Mount Pleasant.)

Left to right: Georgianna Bump, Marcelline Hemingway, Bill Smith, Katy Smith, Ernest, Lucille Dick, and Carl Edgar on the Horton Bay dock, 1920. (Courtesy of the Ernest Hemingway Collection at the John F. Kennedy Presidential Library, Boston.)

The Horton Bay dock and warehouses were popular for social occasions. (Courtesy of Clarke Historical Library, Central Michigan University, Mount Pleasant.)

They were all swimming off the end of the dock. As Nick walked along the rough boards high above the water he heard the double protest of the long springboard and a splash. The water lapped below in the piles.

"Summer People," in *Nick Adams Stories*, 219.

Returning After the War

After his 1917 summer in Michigan, Ernest moved to Kansas City where he worked as a cub reporter for the *Kansas City Star.* He lived for awhile with his Horton Bay friend Carl Edgar and learned all he could about newspaper work and the city. Like all other American newspapers, the *Star* regularly reported events in Europe—especially since the United States had entered the war. Real action was there, Ernest knew, not here in the States. Suspecting his weak left eye would keep him from being a soldier, he chose a different route to get to the war. He signed up for the Red Cross Ambulance Service and waited to be called up. After quitting at the *Star* in April, Ernest arrived back in Oak Park on May 2 for an overnight stay. He was headed to Michigan with Carl Edgar, Bill Smith, and Charles Hopkins for a fishing trip. This trip would be a short one, as no sooner had they got there than a telegram arrived ordering Ernest to report to New York no later than May 8. These few days were all he would see of Michigan that year.

He arrived in New York, then went on to Paris and thence Italy, where he was assigned to a location near the front. While delivering supplies in July, he was injured by an exploding mortar shell and machine gun fire. Amputation of his leg was considered, and he nearly died. Months of slow, painful recovery in a Milan hospital followed, and there he fell in love with his nurse, Agnes von Kurowsky. By January 1919 he had healed enough to go back to Oak Park, where he moved back in with his family and made plans to return to Europe and resume his relationship with Agnes. But that was not to be. In March he received a letter from her ending the relationship, and he was devastated.

Physically and emotionally disabled, he focused, that spring of 1919, on returning to a place when he could heal—northern Michigan. Looking for people to share the experiences, he urged longtime Michigan summer friends, Oak Park classmates, and new friends from Kansas City (Charles Hopkins and Ted Brumback) and the war (Jim Gamble, Bill Horne, and Howell Jenkins) to join him. At this point in his life he no longer stayed with his family at Windemere, instead preferring a tent at the farm or a borrowed room at Horton Bay. This had the added advantage that visiting friends could stay with the Smiths or at Pinehurst, the Dilworths' inn. His friends did come to Michigan, and in 1919 Ernest engineered three major fishing trips—one to Seney in Michigan's Upper Peninsula and two to an area east of Horton Bay called the Pine Barrens. There three rivers (the Black, Sturgeon, and Pigeon) were close to each other and travel between them was easy on the highlands left bare by lumbering. Correspondence between Ernest and his friends reveals much anticipation and then, great fishing success. Gradually the healing began, and though in 1920 there were fewer trips, the ones that did take place were a welcomed distraction and thoroughly enjoyed.

Left to right: Carl "Odgar" Edgar, Katy Smith, Marcelline Hemingway, Bill Horne, Ernest Hemingway, and Bill Smith. Notice the look on Ernest's face as he points his pistol at the cameraman. (Courtesy of the Ernest Hemingway Collection at the John F. Kennedy Presidential Library, Boston.)

And Jim we are going to have a wonderful gang up there. Bill [Smith] who I told you of is a wonder. Then there is Carl Edgar, a Princeton man of the same easy going humorous type as Bill Horne who reads fairy tales and swims and fishes when anyone else wants to. He's been an artillery officer during the late unpleasantness. Carl's coming in July. . . . Bill and I have bumbed together for years and got together on a trip last year before I went overseas. Bill is known as the Master Biologist because some university decorated him with that degree, Carl as the Oil Maggot, because he owns some kind of oil business somewhere . . . and I am the Massive Woodsman. This title entitles me to cut wood and build fires while the Master Biologist and the Maggot lie on their backs and praise my skill. It's a great gang Jim and I know you will like them. At Bill's place is his sister Kate, a rare good scout and good talker and game for any of the parties and Mrs. Charles, Bill's aunt who is one of our own people. Bill's place can't put us all up at once so when Hop [Charles Hopkins] comes up I'll move down to Dilworth's who have the leading house in the four house town of Horton's Bay and have plenty of beds, good rooms in a cottage and cooking that I've been wanting to get to ever since I came back from Italy. Very reasonable rates and the food and accommodations are splendid. We could have a great time Jim. Why can't you come?

Letter to Jim Gamble, April 27, 1919, CMU.

Bill [Smith] and I have camping outfit for 4 men. Tents blankets cooking utensils, camp, grate and so forth. Where we will go will be the Pine Barrens and camp on the Black River. It is wild as the devil and the most wonderful trout fishing you can imagine. All clear—no brush and the trout are in schools. The last time we were over Bill twice caught and landed two at once. Fishing a fly and a grasshopper and there are some hellers too. We can fish all we want and loaf around camp and maybe get a crack at a deer or a bear. . . .

And on the Barrens they [the roads] are fine. Because they're not cut up by traffic at all. You can nearly drive across the Pine Barrens without any road just by compass. It is so free from underbrush.

Gee but we will have a good time. That Barrens Country is the greatest I've ever been in and you know that Bill and you and Barney [Larry Barnet] and I will have *some* time. There are great camping places on the Black and we ought to get some partridges. I can *guarantee you* and Barney both to catch all the trout you want. And Fever [Howell Jenkins] I can sure cook those trout. . . . Bring a camera and any junk you want to. We'll get some great action pictures. . . .

P.S. Bill says to come up Multa Subito and to bring heavy supplies of the grog. Picture us on the Barrens, beside the river with a campfire and the tent and the full moon and a good meal in our bellies smoking a pill and with a good bottle of grog. There will be some good singing.

Letter to Howell Jenkins, July 26, 1919, in *Selected Letters*, 26.

Next page: Ernest with his Italian beret, high-laced boots, and fly rod case at the Pine Barrens. Note the stumps and wide-open spaces left by lumbering a generation earlier.
(Courtesy of the Ernest Hemingway Collection at the John F. Kennedy Presidential Library, Boston.)

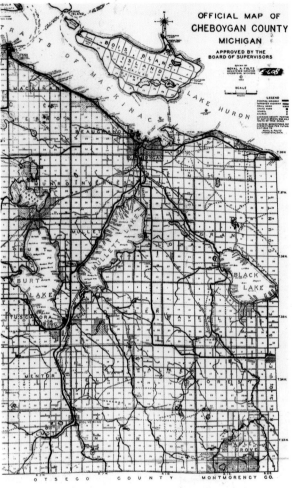

Above: The Pine Barrens were located south of Black and Mullet lakes and east of Wolverine. (Author's collection.)

Hemingway's favorite way to prepare fish was to roll them in cornmeal and then fry them in Crisco while basting slowly with bacon slices. Ernest is holding the frying pan while Bill Smith and Charles Hopkins look on. (Courtesy of the Ernest Hemingway Collection at the John F. Kennedy Presidential Library, Boston.)

Left: Bill Smith was one of Ernest's best friends at Horton Bay. This photo shows him on a dock there. (Courtesy of the Ernest Hemingway Collection at the John F. Kennedy Presidential Library, Boston.)

Above, left to right: Carl Edgar, Charles Hopkins, Ernest Hemingway, and Bill Smith. This photo was likely taken on their way to fish in Michigan in early May 1918. Days later Ernest would be off to serve in the Red Cross Ambulance service in Italy. (Courtesy of the Ernest Hemingway Collection at the John F. Kennedy Presidential Library, Boston.)

We had a marvelous time this trip. Brummy [Ted Brumback] and Jacques [Jock Pentecost] and the Fever and a new guy named Dick Smale. Brum can play the mandolin wonderfully and in the evening he would play after supper in the dusk and 'side the camp fire. And before we went to sleep we'd all be curled up around the fire. . . . We rented a car and trailer for a week. Jock and I took some darby fish. . . . Didn't we rate a great moon the first of last week? It was great in camp lying all rolled up in the blankets after the fire had died down to coals and the men were asleep and looking at the moon and thinking long long thoughts. In Sicily they say it makes you queer to sleep with the moon on your face. Moon struck. Maybe that's what ails me.

Letter to Grace Quinlan, August 8, 1920, in *Selected Letters*, 35.

Hemingway and friends during their August 1919 fishing trip on the Black River. *Left to right:* unknown, Howell "Fever" Jenkins, Ernest, and Bill Smith. (Courtesy of the Ernest Hemingway Collection at the John F. Kennedy Presidential Library, Boston.)

Fishing camp on the Pine Barrens. Hemingway is standing on the right. (Courtesy of the Ernest Hemingway Collection at the John F. Kennedy Presidential Library, Boston.)

Not all roads on the Pine Barrens were as good as Hemingway tried to convince his friends they were. (Courtesy of the Ernest Hemingway Collection at the John F. Kennedy Presidential Library, Boston.)

Hemingway always seemed to have good luck fishing at the Barrens. (Courtesy of the Ernest Hemingway Collection at the John F. Kennedy Presidential Library, Boston.)

SENEY AND "BIG TWO-HEARTED RIVER"

Perhaps Hemingway's best and most famous short story is "Big Two-Hearted River." The story describes a Nick Adams fishing excursion near Seney in Michigan's Upper Peninsula. As was often the case, Hemingway used his own experiences as inspiration for this story. In late August 1919, Ernest traveled with high school classmate Jock Pentecost and Al Walker to Seney, where they fished the Fox River. (Hemingway admitted later that he used the name of the nearby Two Hearted River for the title, rather than the Fox, because it was "pure poetry.") Early drafts of the story included the two other fishermen, but as the story developed only Nick remained. The real trip was a test of Ernest's endurance. It would involve significant hiking and stream wading on his injured leg. It is said that when he got off the train at Seney, the brakeman told the engineer to wait as there was a "cripple" who needed extra time. That cripple was Ernest. Physically he was slowly mending, but his injuries caused him constant pain and stiffness. Emotionally he was better but facing the end of a summer season in Michigan and

Hemingway in 1919 after returning from World War I. (Courtesy of the Ernest Hemingway Collection at the John F. Kennedy Presidential Library, Boston.)

an uncertain fall. The story "Big Two-Hearted River" describes a recuperative and deliberate fishing experience by someone who is obviously suffering. In it, returning to fishing and remembering the comfort its rituals provide helps Nick Adams begin to heal himself.

Jock and Al Walker and I just got back from Seney. The Fox is priceless. The big fox is about 4 or five times as large as the Black and has ponds 40 feet across. The little Fox is about the size of the Black and lousy with them. Jock caught one that weighed 2 lbs. 15 and a half of the inches. I got one 15 inches on the fly! Also one 14 inches. We caught about 200 and were gone a week. We were only about 15 miles from the Pictured Rocks on Lake Superior. Gad that is great country.

Letter to Howell Jenkins, September 15, 1919, in *Selected Letters*, 28.

Al Walker. (Courtesy of Jim Sanford and Clarke Historical Library, Central Michigan University, Mount Pleasant.)

Ernest and Jock Pentecost, 1919. (Courtesy of the Ernest Hemingway Collection at the John F. Kennedy Presidential Library, Boston.)

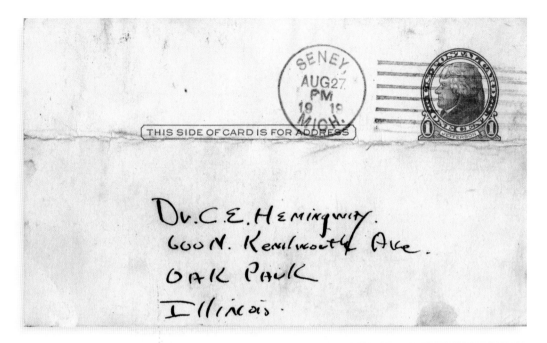

Ernest describes his trip in this postcard sent to his father from Seney. (Courtesy of Clarke Historical Library, Central Michigan University, Mount Pleasant.)

We caught some brook trout 1 3/4 lbs. up here. 10 miles north in Schoolcraft Co. Yesterday I caught 27 smallest nine inches. Lots of deer and game here. Going home to Horton's [Bay] now. Jock Pentecost Al Walker and I. Hope to see you up this September. Have been out a week.

Letter to Clarence Hemingway, August 27, 1919, CMU.

I sat in a corner with the afternoon light coming in over my shoulder and wrote in the notebook. The waiter brought me a café crème and I drank half of it when it cooled and left it on the table when I wrote. When I stopped writing I did not want to leave the river where I could see in the pool, its surface pushing and swelling against the resistance of the log driven piles of the bridge. The story was about coming back from the war but there was no mention of the war in it. But in the morning the river would be there and I must make it and the country and all that would happen. There were days ahead to be doing that each day.

"Hunger Was Good Discipline," in *A Moveable Feast*, 76.

Top: Railroad bridge over the Fox River at Seney. Nick Adams looks down from this bridge in "Big Two-Hearted River." (Courtesy of Seney Historical Museum, Seney.)

Above: Fox River with high water level in springtime. The water would have been much lower when Hemingway was there in August. (Courtesy of Seney Historical Museum, Seney.)

Hemingway in uniform with cane, 1919. (Courtesy of the Ernest Hemingway Collection at the John F. Kennedy Presidential Library, Boston.)

The train went on up the track out of sight, around one of the hills of burned timber. Nick sat down on the bundle of canvas and bedding the baggage man had pitched out of the door of the baggage car. There was no town, nothing but the rails and the burned-over country. The thirteen saloons that had lined the one street of Seney had not left a trace. The foundations of the Mansion House hotel stuck up above the ground. The stone was chipped and split by the fire. It was all that was left of the town of Seney. Even the surface had been burned off the ground.

"Big Two-Hearted River," in *Nick Adams Stories*, 177.

Looking east at Seney. The Fox River and railroad bridge are in the foreground. (Courtesy of Seney Historical Museum, Seney.)

Looking west at Seney. The effect of logging is evident in the treeless landscape. (Courtesy of Seney Historical Museum, Seney.)

The Grondin Hotel burned shortly before Hemingway arrived in 1919. It is likely its foundations were still visible when he arrived to fish. (Courtesy of Seney Historical Museum, Seney.)

Nick walked back up the ties to where his pack lay in the cinders beside the railway track. He was happy. He adjusted the pack harness around the bundle, pulling straps tight, slung the pack on his back, got his arms through the shoulder straps and took some of the pull off his shoulders by leaning his forehead against the wide band of the tumpline. Still it was too heavy. It was much too heavy. He had his leather rod-case in his hand and leaning forward to keep the weight of the pack high on his shoulders he walked along the road that paralleled the railway track, leaving the burned town behind in the heat, and then turned off around a hill with a high, fire-scarred hill on either side of the road that went back into the country.

"Big Two-Hearted River," in *Nick Adams Stories*, 178.

This page: Ernest with his fishing gear, likely at the Pine Barrens, 1920. (Courtesy of the Ernest Hemingway Collection at the John F. Kennedy Presidential Library, Boston.)

Next page: Hemingway pretending to hop a freight car, 1915 or 1916. Note the amount of gear he carried. (Courtesy of the Ernest Hemingway Collection at the John F. Kennedy Presidential Library, Boston.)

Hemingway splitting firewood for the campfire, Pine Barrens, 1920. (Courtesy of the Ernest Hemingway Collection at the John F. Kennedy Presidential Library, Boston.)

With the ax he split off a bright slab of pine from one of the stumps and split it into pegs for the tent. He wanted them long and solid to hold it in the ground. With the tent unpacked and spread on the ground, the pack leaning against a jack pine, looked much smaller. Nick tied the rope that served the tent for a ridgepole to the trunk of one of the pine trees and pulled the tent up off the ground with the other end of the rope and tied it to the other pine. The tent hung on the rope like a canvas blanket on a clothesline. . . . Inside the tent the light came through the brown canvas. It smelled pleasantly of canvas. Already there was something mysterious and home-like. Nick was happy as he crawled inside the tent.

"Big Two-Hearted River," in *Nick Adams Stories*, 183.

Note how closely Ernest's equipment resembles Nick Adams's—including the flour sack and bottle hanging around his neck for grasshoppers. (Courtesy of the Ernest Hemingway Collection at the John F. Kennedy Presidential Library, Boston.)

He started down the stream, holding his rod, the bottle of grasshoppers hung from his neck by a thong tied in half hitches around the neck of the bottle. His landing net hung by a hook from his belt. Over his shoulder was a long flour sack tied at each corner into an ear. The cord went over his shoulder. The sack flapped against his legs. Nick felt awkward and professionally happy with all his equipment hanging from him. The grasshopper bottle swung against his chest. In his shirt the breast pockets bulged against him with the lunch and his fly book.

"Big Two-Hearted River," in *Nick Adams Stories*, 190.

Ernest carefully landing a trout on his hike to Michigan, 1915 or 1916. (Courtesy of the Ernest Hemingway Collection at the John F. Kennedy Presidential Library, Boston.)

He stepped into the stream. It was a shock. His trousers clung tight to his legs. His shoes felt the gravel. The water was rising cold shock. Rushing, the current sucked against his legs. Where he stepped in, the water was over his knees. He waded with the current. The gravel slid under his shoes. He looked down at the swirl of water below each leg and tipped up the bottle to get a grasshopper.

"Big Two-Hearted River," in *Nick Adams Stories*, 190.

Ernest walking through a clearing on his way to Walloon Lake, 1915 or 1916. (Courtesy of the Ernest Hemingway Collection at the John F. Kennedy Presidential Library, Boston.)

Living in Petoskey, Fall 1919

Back from his fishing trip to Seney, in the fall of 1919 Ernest Hemingway was at a crossroads. He had returned from the war months before and had enjoyed a healing summer filled with fishing and friends, but it was now time to get on with his life. His Horton Bay friends were leaving for their homes and jobs, the summer resorts were closing for the season, and his parents were hoping he would attend college, perhaps to become a doctor practicing with his father. They were quietly worried that he would never settle on a profession and become a failure. He knew he could give newspaper work a try as he had seven months of professional journalism experience working at the *Kansas City Star*. But deep down he knew he really wanted to try writing stories. He did not need to earn a wage immediately. An insurance policy paid enough for his basic needs for the time being. Writing it would be then. The question was, where would he go to write? He chose to stay in Michigan.

The first week of October Ernest rode with Bill Smith to his parents' Oak Park home where he explained that he wanted to focus on his writing and then returned immediately north to the Dilworths'. When Pinehurst closed for the season he left Horton Bay and secured a second-story room at Eva Potter's boardinghouse on State Street in Petoskey. The sparsely furnished, $8-a-week room did not include meals, so Ernest took them at local diners and with friends. He had spent time in Petoskey before, but this was different. In the summer the town was filled with tourists and resorters, the water in the bay blue, and the days filled with sunlight and warmth. But fall in Petoskey was not the same—especially this fall. It was quiet: the wind cutting and the water a cold, icy gray. He wandered the streets, hanging out at the local barbershop, the train station, and the new Carnegie Library. He sought out his Petoskey friends.

And, most importantly to him, he wrote. Sitting at his desk using the typewriter he had borrowed from Bill Smith, he faithfully worked on stories designed for the popular magazines of the day.

Next page: Formerly Eva Potter's boardinghouse and now a private residence. Hemingway's room was upstairs and in the front. (Courtesy of Clarke Historical Library, Central Michigan University, Mount Pleasant.)

He even sought the advice of Edwin Balmer, an editor of *Redbook*, who was staying at Bay View. Balmer thought one story set in a Chicago Italian restaurant showed promise and suggested he change the title from "The Woppian Way" to "The Passing of Pickles McCarthy." But he never did get his stories "right," and all he received were rejection notices. Eventually he and Bill Smith, exchanging letters, decided to try capturing some of the Horton Bay people they knew in short character sketches. These writings, though not published in Hemingway's lifetime, showed the beginning of the style for which he became famous and were his first professional use of Michigan people and places in his fiction.

When not writing or wandering, he spent his time with friends like Edwin "Dutch" Pailthorp, Luman Ramsdell, Marjorie Bump, and Grace Quinlan. Dutch was an outgoing, thin, red-haired friend

who had just left the University of Michigan for medical reasons. The son of a prominent lawyer, Dutch knew how to find drink in this prohibition dry town. That fall Ernest and Dutch made a barrel of hard cider (using raisins to help ferment it) that was consumed at a secret November party held at the Ramsdell's Bay View cottage. (Luman Ramsdell was the son of the local doctor.) It was there that Ernest met Irene Goldstein (Gordon), who was to become his friend and tennis partner. She was almost identical to him in age and in wit. The younger Petoskey girls (Marje and Grace) were simply fun to be around. They were a willing audience and they provided distractions for him. Fourteen-year-old Grace, known for her dark hair and eyes, was nicknamed "Sister Luke." She lived a couple of houses away from Mrs. Potter's, and Ernest enjoyed talking in her kitchen over a bowl of popcorn. Marjorie Bump lived just around the corner. She was a cute, red-haired, dimpled thirteen-year-old when she first met Hemingway in 1917 while she was staying with relatives at Horton Bay and working at the Dilworths' Pinehurst Cottage as a summer waitress. It is said that during the summer of 1919 he smoked cigarettes on the Dilworths' porch while waiting

for her to get off work and that occasionally they would share picnics at the point at Horton Bay. Now that he was living close by in Petoskey, it was common to see him waiting to walk her and her sister, Georgianna, home after school. They shared the latest gossip with him and he provided advice on a host of matters. The stories he told of Italy were entertaining, if not always true. But Petoskey was and is a small town and this limping war veteran, who dressed roughly and paid attention to the younger schoolgirls, must have raised some suspicions.

For the most part, however, it was an uneventful fall for Ernest and his friends. On November 11 (Armistice Day) he delivered a speech about his war experiences at the local high school, which mirrored earlier ones he had given in Oak Park. In December he was invited to talk to the Ladies Aid Society at the Petoskey Public Library on Mitchell Street. To this event he wore his Italian cloak with silver clasp and his polished cordovan boots (rather than the sheepskin-lined black leather jacket and cloth cap he was most often seen in when walking Petoskey's streets). Mrs. Harriet Connable, wife of the head of F. W. Woolworth in Canada, was in attendance

Left: Marjorie Bump in Petoskey, November or December 1919. While the true nature of their relationship is unclear, Hemingway did use her name and elements of their friendship in the short stories "The End of Something" and "Three Day Blow." (Courtesy of the Ernest Hemingway Collection at the John F. Kennedy Presidential Library, Boston.)

Above: Petoskey High School was only blocks from Hemingway's boardinghouse, and he was frequently seen there walking friends home after school. (Author's collection.)

that night and afterward approached Hemingway about coming to Toronto for the winter to serve as a companion to her disabled son, Ralph, while she and her husband traveled to Florida. With few other prospects, Hemingway agreed and left Petoskey in late December. After a short obligatory holiday stay in Oak Park, he spent the next months in Toronto, where he and Dutch Pailthorp (who was working temporarily for Woolworth's there and staying at the YMCA) spent time with Ralph, taking him to boxing matches and hockey games. By June, Hemingway, had returned to Horton Bay to spend another summer in northern Michigan.

Hemingway in Petoskey, November or December 1919. (Courtesy of Little Traverse Region Historical Museum, Petoskey.)

SOLDIERS TALK AT HIGH SCHOOL

TELL PUPILS OF THEIR WAR EXPERIENCES.

Grade Schools Also Hear Interesting Talks From Men Who Served With the Army Overseas.

At the high school yesterday Hemenway, of Oak Park, Ill., who was with the Allied armies in Italy, told the high school students some of his war experiences, as a part of the Armistice Day activities.

Mr. Hemenway spent the summer with his parents at their Walloon Lake summer home, and during the autumn has been in Petoskey. He was badly wounded during the fighting in Italy and believes Northern Michigan climate is aiding him to recover his health.

Prof. Charles Kuttler, who was with the forestry section of the U. S. Engineers in France, told some of his experiences during the war. Mr. Kuttler also spoke at Sheridan street school. At Lincoln school James Niles gave a most interesting talk to the children, while at Central school Mr. Van Every, a returned soldier, talked on the war.

The Petoskey Public Library building where Ernest spoke to the Ladies Aid Society in December 1919. (Courtesy of Little Traverse Region Historical Museum, Petoskey.)

Petoskey Evening News, November 12, 1919. (Courtesy of Little Traverse Region Historical Museum, Petoskey.)

Had a very rough and stormy trip up on the Missouri. She got away about 4 p/m and into Petoskey at midnight. Cold and stormy. I was not sick however.

Spent the night at the Cushman [Hotel] and went up and saw the Bumps in the morning and went to the Presbt. Church with old Mrs. Bump. Have a room located at 602 State Street where I wish you would forward my mail and anything else. It is small but heated and gives me a place to work. Monday caught the train in to Boyne Falls and thence to Boyne City and so via Wesley to here last night. Brought the typewriter from Charles's Shanty and am departing with it and my other worldly goods to Petoskey on Thursday—probably taking the same route I came out on. This afternoon I worked out the new front part of the "Woppian Way" that Balmer wanted me to do and will have it in shape to start on its travels as soon as I am settled in Petoskey. I typed off the new part this afternoon. It was snowing a little this evening and the only amusement offered is an Evangelical revival. There is some doubt as to whether I will attend.

Since leaving Oak Park have read a volume of stories by Guy de Maupassant one by Balzac, the Larger Testament of Francois Villon, Richard Yes and Nay by Maurice Hewlett and little novels of Italy also by Hewlett. These are all things that are further along in college than Marcelline ever achieved so you see I have not been entirely idle.

Thank you very much for helping me so much and give my love to mother and the kids.

Letter to Clarence Hemingway, October 28, 1919, CMU.

HORTON BAY WEDDING

After spending the summer of 1920 at Horton Bay, Ernest moved to Chicago, where he lived with Bill Smith's brother, Y. K. Smith. That fall, Katy Smith invited a friend of hers from St. Louis, Hadley Richardson, to a party held at the apartment and at it she and Ernest began a relationship that would result in marriage months later. Ernest was not keen on a big Oak Park wedding, and Hadley, who had recently lost her parents, likewise did not want a large formal ceremony in St. Louis. Ernest suggested they marry at Horton Bay in northern Michigan and she agreed. The date was set for September 3, 1921, and arrangements were made—with the help of his Petoskey schoolgirl friend, Grace Quinlan, who was asked to help secure a minister. Ernest arrived from Chicago on August 28 and, after a quick fishing trip to the Sturgeon River, showed up at Horton Bay, where he and the groomsmen stayed at the Dilworths'. When Hadley arrived she stayed with her friend Katy Smith at the Charles's farm.

The wedding day went smoothly, with the seldom-used Methodist church decorated with local wildflowers. The wedding party gathered in the afternoon behind the Horton Bay store before going next door to the church where, it was noted, Ernest had difficultly kneeling because of his war injuries. The thirty guests included locals and a few friends and relatives from the couple's hometowns. A wedding meal was served afterward at the Dilworths', and the couple was taken via John Kotesky's Model T to the Walloon Lake shore at Longfield Farm, whence Ernest rowed Hadley across to Windemere, where they spent their two-week honeymoon. Suffering from colds, they were said to have slept on the floor in front of the warm fireplace on a mattress pulled from one of the beds. Ernest took her to Petoskey to meet his friends, most of whom were girls. It was an awkward experience for Hadley and for the admiring schoolgirls. Although the marriage initially was a happy one, it is clear that Ernest realized it would bring an end to his carefree summers with friends in Michigan.

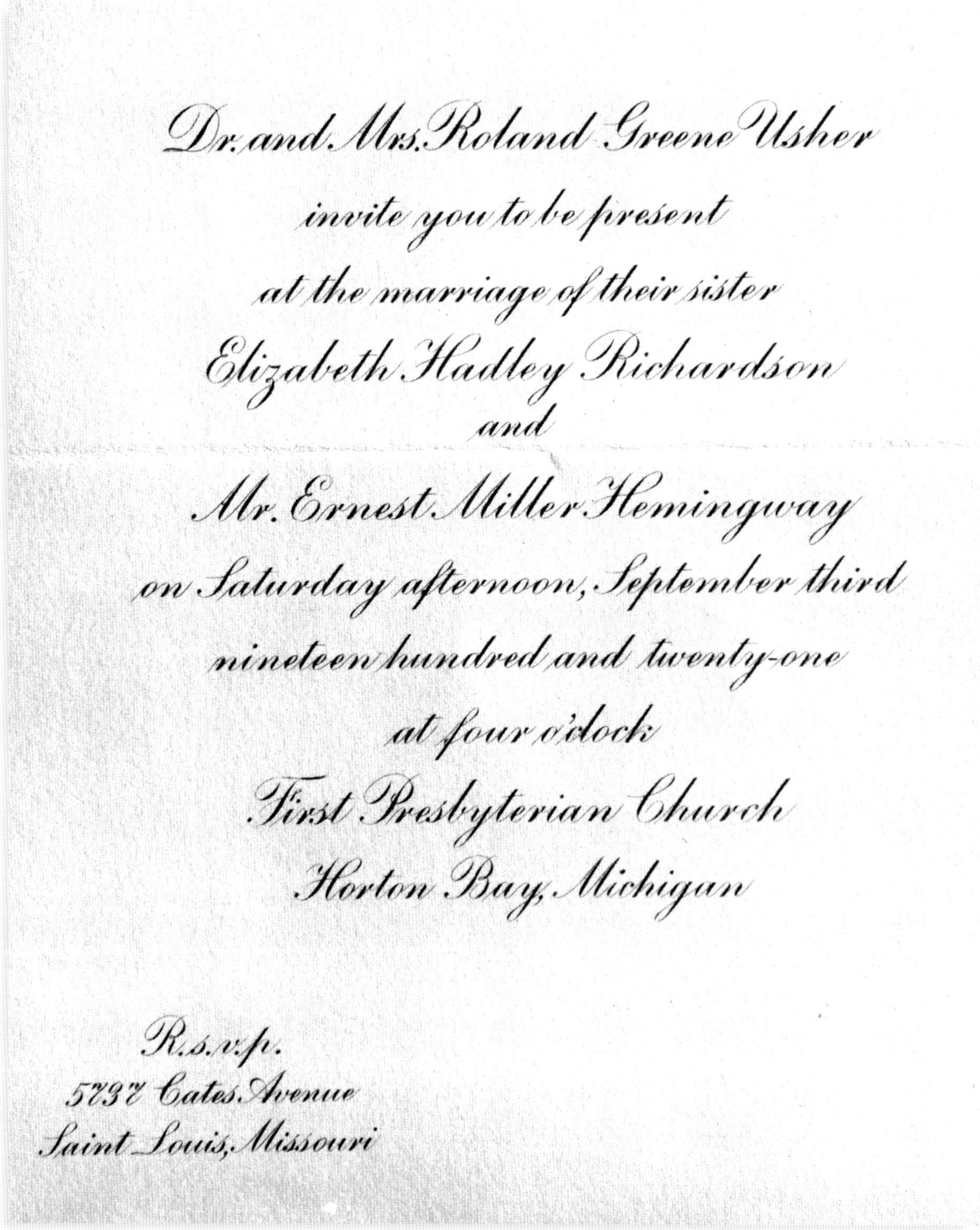

The wedding invitation mistakenly indicates the ceremony will take place at a Horton Bay Presbyterian church when in reality it was to be at a Methodist one. The church did not hold regular services at that time and has since been demolished. (Courtesy of Little Traverse Region Historical Museum, Petoskey.)

Dr. and Mrs. Roland Greene Usher

invite you to be present

at the marriage of their sister

Elizabeth Hadley Richardson

and

Mr. Ernest Miller Hemingway

on Saturday afternoon, September third

nineteen hundred and twenty-one

at four o'clock

First Presbyterian Church

Horton Bay, Michigan

R.s.v.p.
5737 Cates Avenue
Saint Louis, Missouri

Wish to hell I was going Nort [north] when you men do. Doubt if I get up this summer—Jo Eezus [Jesus], sometimes I get to thinking about the Sturgeon and Black during the nocturnal [night] and damn near go cuckoo. . . . May have to give it up for something I want more but that does not keep me from loving it with everything I have. Dats de way tings are. Guy loves a couple of or three steams all his life and loves 'em better than anything in the world—falls in love with a girl and the goddamn streams can dry up for all he cares. Only the hell of it is that all that country has as bad a hold on me as ever—there's as much pull this spring as there ever was—and you know how it's always been—just don't think about it at all daytime, but at night it comes and ruins me—and I can't go.

Letter to Bill Smith, April 28, 1921, in *Selected Letters*, 47.

Above: Horton Bay as it looked in 1921. (Courtesy of Little Traverse Region Historical Museum, Petoskey.)

Below: While work prevented him from doing so, Ernest longed to return to the Sturgeon and Black rivers during the summer of 1921. He did manage to sneak in a brief trip to the Sturgeon immediately before his wedding. (Courtesy of Clarke Historical Library, Central Michigan University, Mount Pleasant.)

Hemingway in 1921 before his wedding to Hadley Richardson. (Courtesy of the Ernest Hemingway Collection at the John F. Kennedy Presidential Library, Boston.)

Hadley Richardson was twenty-nine at the time of the wedding. Ernest inflated his age from the actual twenty-two to twenty-three on the wedding license. (Courtesy of the Ernest Hemingway Collection at the John F. Kennedy Presidential Library, Boston.)

Suppose you want to hear about Hadley—well her nickname is Hash—she's a wonderful tennis player, best pianist I ever heard and a sort of a terribly fine article. Spite of the clippings prophesying a big wedding in the fall in St. Louis, we're going to fool them and be married at the Bay in that small, trick church there. Then going to kinda bum around for three weeks. . . . The date hasn't been set for the wedding, but it'll be in early Sept.—some time the first week. . . . I can't invite a big lot of people because we're having it Up North to get away from that sort of thing.

Letter to Grace Quinlan, July 21, 1921, in *Selected Letters*, 51.

Ernest and his groomsmen. *Left to right:* Jock Pentecost, Howell Jenkins, unknown, Dutch Pailthorp, Ernest Hemingway, Bill Smith, Bill Horne, Carl Edgar, and Luman Ramsdell
(Courtesy of the Ernest Hemingway Collection at the John F. Kennedy Presidential Library, Boston.)

The bride and groom with his family. *Left to right:* Carol, Ursula, Hadley, Ernest, Grace, Leicester, and Clarence Hemingway. (Courtesy of the Ernest Hemingway Collection at the John F. Kennedy Presidential Library, Boston.)

Why I'm going to leave here [Chicago] the 27th of August and get up North the next morning and probably tear right out for the Sturgeon for the last three days of the fishing season. They close it up on the main [branch] on the first of Sept. and I haven't had any for so long that I am starved and crazy for it. Then I'll be back and standing by til the 3rd when heavy marriage occurs. Outa be a fairly high grade occasion, be a pretty good gang there. Not many people, but a lot of the people we like. I'll be trying to get into Petorskey [sic] to see you before der Tag. . . . Oh Yes. How about ministers, preachers, priests, or prelates?? In your wide and diverse acquaintances can you recommend a capable minister to perform the ceremony? Hash says she does not care particularly what breed of priest it is, but prefers one that does not wear a celluloid collar or chaw tobacco. We thought we could lay hold of Bishop Tuttle for St. Louis that summers at Harbor point, but he may be gone by then. Remember that when selecting this priest that he's gotta be able to read and be dignified. Dignity's what we're going to pay this here prelate for, we don't want no evangelist that's liable to shout out, "Praise be the Lord" and start rolling on the floor during a critical part of the ceremony. Presbyterian preferred, or else Episcopal, doesn't make the slightest difference to me. What's the local prelate situation? Give me a brief resume. Huh? Pick me a prelate.

Letter to Grace Quinlan, August 19, 1921, in *Selected Letters*, 54.

Ernest stayed at the Dilworths' Pinehurst Cottage before the wedding, and a chicken dinner was served there after the ceremony. (Courtesy of Clarke Historical Library, Central Michigan University, Mount Pleasant.)

ERNEST M. HEMMINGWAY
WEDS ST. LOUIS GIRL IN
HORTON BAY CEREMONY.

At a pretty wedding at Horton's Bay Saturday afternoon, Miss Hadley Richardson, of St. Louis, became the bride of Ernest Miller Hemmingway, of Oak Park, Ill. Rev. William J. Datson, of Petoskey, performed the ceremony. There was a large number of guests, mostly from St. Louis and Chicago, and those from Petoskey were Edwin Pailthorp and Luman Ramsdell.

After a month's honeymoon at Walloon Lake Mr. and Mrs. Hemmingway will go to Chicago for a while, after which sojourn they will go to Italy for the winter. Mr. Hemmingway was a lieutenant in the Italian army for several years during the world war, and was decorated for bravery by the Italian government. He is well known and greatly liked in Italy.

Left: Dr. and Mrs. Hemingway after the wedding. (Courtesy of the Ernest Hemingway Collection at the John F. Kennedy Presidential Library, Boston.)

Above: Petoskey Evening News, September 1921. It's interesting that even the wedding article includes misinformation about Ernest's Italian experience and his future plans. (Courtesy of Little Traverse Region Historical Museum, Petoskey.)

He had been in swimming and was washing his feet in the wash bowl after having walked up the hill. The room was hot and Dutch and Luman were both standing around looking nervous. Nick got a clean suit of underwear, clean silk socks, new garters, a white shirt and collar out from the drawer of the bureau and put them on. He stood in front of the mirror and tied his tie. . . . Dutch went out for a corkscrew and came in and opened the bottle. . . . Nick took a couple of swallows. He loved whiskey. Nick pulled on his trousers. He wasn't thinking at all. Horny Bill, Art Meyer, and the Ghee were dressing upstairs.

"Wedding Day," in *Nick Adams Stories*, 231.

After the wedding was over they got into John Kotesky's Ford and drove over the hill road to the lake. Nick paid John Kotesky five dollars and Kotesky helped him carry the bags down to the rowboat. They both shook hands with Kotesky and then his Ford went back up along the road. They could hear it for a long time. Nick could not find the oars where his father had hidden them for him in the plum trees back of the ice house and Helen waited for him down at the boat. Finally he found them and carried them down to the shore. It was a long row across the lake. The night was hot and depressing. Neither of them talked much. A few people had spoiled the wedding. Nick rowed hard when they were near shore and shot the boat up on the sandy beach. . . . Nick unlocked the door and then went back to the boat to get the bags. He lit the lamps and they looked through the cottage together.

"Wedding Day," in *Nick Adams Stories*, 232.

When he married he lost Bill Smith, Odgar, the Ghee, all the old gang. . . . He had built it all up. Bill had never fished before they met. Everyplace they had been together. The Black, the Sturgeon, the Pine Barrens, the Upper Minnie, all the little streams. Most about the fishing he and Bill had discovered together. They worked on the farm and fished and took long trips in the woods from June to October. Bill always quit his job every spring. So did he. . . . They were all married to fishing.

"On Writing," in *Nick Adams Stories*, 234.

Epilogue

After his Windemere honeymoon ended in 1921, Ernest Hemingway would only physically return to northern Michigan once—a one-night stay in Petoskey twenty-six years later. That was when, in September 1947, he and his friend and driver, Toby Bruce, were headed to Sun Valley, Idaho. No longer was he the innocent child vacationing with his parents or even the boastful but inexperienced young man with lots of charm and stories. Instead he was a bearded celebrity, overweight at 265 pounds with a blood pressure that had risen dangerously high, to 215 over 125. He was married to his fourth wife, and his novels *The Sun Also Rises, A Farewell to Arms,* and *For Whom the Bell Tolls* had brought him wealth and international fame. In five years he would write *The Old Man and the Sea* and then win the Nobel Prize for Literature. In fourteen he would pull his shotgun's trigger and end his own life. But on this September day he had just learned that his friend, Katy Smith, had been killed in a tragic automobile accident that also injured her husband, the author John dos Passos. Did that stir up memories of teasing her at the Horton Bay dock and lazy afternoons at the Charles's farm? He had just been offered the huge sum of $75,000 each for the movie rights to four of his stories by the man who produced the hit movie based on his story "The Killers," staring Eva Gardner and Burt Lancaster. One wonders if that story, in early drafts set firmly in Petoskey, was on Ernest's mind as he pulled into town or if he recalled staring at a blank sheet of paper while bundled up in his cold room at Mrs. Potter's rooming house. This Ernest Hemingway, who burst into the law office of his old friend, Dutch Pailthorp, and who then rushed down the street to see Irene Gordon, was far removed from the newlywed who left Michigan in 1921. Clearly he had left Michigan behind and moved on. Or had he?

When Ernest left Petoskey with his new bride that September of 1921, they went to Chicago, where a job and small apartment

For Dutch Pailthorp
to whom I told this
story in the winter of
1919-20 in Petoskey,
Michigan
from his old
friend
Ernie Hemingway.

Edwin "Dutch" Pailthorp became friends with Hemingway in the fall of 1919, and Ernest visited with him when he returned to Petoskey in 1947. This inscription is in Pailthorp's copy of *A Farewell to Arms* and is on display at the Little Traverse History Museum at Petoskey. The article is from the *Petoskey Evening News* on Saturday, September 27, 1947. (Courtesy of Little Traverse Region Historical Museum, Petoskey.)

Hemingway Visits City

Ernest Hemingway, noted author who was a Walloon Lake and Petoskey resident during his youth, stopped overnight here enroute from Florida to Sun Valley, Idaho.

According to an old friend, Edwin G. Pailthorp, this was Mr. Hemingway's first visit to Petoskey since he spent the winter of 1919-1920 here.

"He still owns the family home on Walloon Lake and wanted to take a look at it," Mr. Pailthorp said. "He was more than pleased to find Northern Michigan much as he remembered it from many years ago."

Mr. Hemingway, after long service as a war correspondent, now has his residence in Havana, Cuba. He arrived Thursday and left Friday shortly after noon, accompanied by Otto Bruce, a former secretary who is a Key West, Fla., businessman.

awaited him and Hadley. Months later, longing for Europe and depending on her small trust fund and the money he made writing occasional articles for the *Toronto Star*, they moved to Paris. In the company of other Lost Generation expatriates, the couple enjoyed the City of Lights and Ernest spent as much time as he could writing what he wanted to write—stories. It was there that he made use of, rather than ignored, his relationship with Michigan. He discovered Nick Adams, remembered with precise detail the Michigan places he knew so well, and perfected the style that revolutionized American literature. Short stories set there were not only written but sold and published. He discovered that his stash of Michigan memories was not only large but useful. A few Nick Adams stories turned into several and then many. When he wanted to break a contract with his first publisher, he wrote a novel mocking the style of its leading author. That novel, *The Torrents of Spring,* is set in the diners and on the cold winter streets of Petoskey. As Hemingway's life experiences took him to new wars, to Africa, Key West, Spain, Cuba, and the American West, Michigan went with him. It shows up again in stories like "The Snows of Kilimanjaro," where he gives an elaborate description of the Bacons' homestead—something he saw as a boy thirty years before. In *True at First Light* (unpublished during his lifetime but written in the 1950s) he remembers the sweet taste of cider from the Horton Bay cider mill, and in *A Moveable Feast*, the manuscript he was working on when he died in 1961, he recalls the writing of those first, true Michigan stories. No, Ernest Hemingway never really did leave northern Michigan. Instead, he carried it with him and gifted it to the rest of the world.

Hemingway's first novel, *The Torrents of Spring*, was published 1926 when Ernest and Hadley were living in Paris. It is set in Petoskey and contains numerous references to places he frequented during his time there. (Courtesy of Little Traverse Region Historical Museum, Petoskey.)

THE TORRENTS OF SPRING

A ROMANTIC NOVEL IN HONOR OF THE PASSING OF A GREAT RACE

ERNEST HEMINGWAY

AUTHOR OF "IN OUR TIME"

THE TORRENTS OF SPRING

By
Ernest Hemingway

Ernest Hemingway, who in serious moments admits no special literary allegiances, here departs for a time from his own characteristic style, joins the so-called "Chicago School of Literature," allows himself to fall under the influence of Sherwood Anderson, *et al.*, and shows that he can do it too.

While living in Paris recently he decided that it would be well to write the story of Yogi Johnson of the pump factory in Petoskey, Michigan, and of his friend, Scripps O'Neil, who married the elderly waitress, Diana, of Brown's Beanery (Best by Test). Diana, like several other mid-western heroines, tried to hold her husband by repeatedly luring him to her with bait dug from *The Manchester Guardian*, *The Mentor*, and *The American Mercury*. Her noble and tragic effort, and its result, find in Mr. Hemingway a broadly sympathetic interpreter. The author's notes "to the reader, not the printer" add coherence unusual in a tale of this sort, and incidentally supply us with information regarding the recent movements of himself and his friends, Mr. Dos Passos and Mr. Scott Fitzgerald, in the famous Latin Quarter.

Of special importance to the followers of literary schools are the chapters on "Red and Black Laughter" and the "Making and Marring of Americans."

CHARLES SCRIBNER'S SONS

BIBLIOGRAPHY

Baker, Carlos. *Ernest Hemingway: A Life Story.* New York: Charles Scribner's Sons, 1969.

Browne, Arline M. *In the Wake of the Topinabee.* Lancaster, CA: Hubbard Map Service, 1967.

Buske, Morris. "Dad, Are We There Yet?" *Michigan History Magazine* 83 (March/April 1999): 16–27.

Byron, M. Christine, and Thomas R Wilson. *Vintage Views of the Charlevoix-Petoskey Region.* Traverse City, MI: Petoskey Publishing, 2005.

Cappel, Constance. *Hemingway in Michigan.* Petoskey, MI: Little Traverse Historical Society, 1999.

Dunbar, Willis. *All Aboard! A History of Railroads in Michigan.* Grand Rapids, MI: William Eerdmans, 1969.

Early Postcard Views of Harbor Springs. Harbor Springs, MI: Harbor Springs Area Historical Society, 2006.

Erb, Mary, Cynthia Hermann, and Charles Schloff. *Walloon Yesterdays.* Petoskey, MI: Mitchell Graphics, 2003.

Griffin, Peter. *Along with Youth: Hemingway; The Early Years.* New York: Oxford University Press, 1985.

A Guide to the Health, Pleasure, and Fishing Resorts of Northern Michigan Reached by the Grand Rapids and Indiana Railroad. Grand Rapids, MI, 1879.

Hemingway, Ernest. *Complete Short Stories of Ernest Hemingway.* New York: Scribners, 1987.

———. *Ernest Hemingway: Selected Letters, 1917–1961.* Edited by Carlos Baker. New York: Scribners, 1981.

———. *A Moveable Feast.* New York: Charles Scribner's Sons, 1964.

———. *The Nick Adams Stories.* New York: Simon and Schuster, 1972.

———. *The Torrents of Spring.* New York: Simon and Schuster, 1998.

Hemingway, Leicester. *My Brother, Ernest Hemingway.* New York: World Publishing, 1962.

Hilton, George. *Lake Michigan Passenger Streamers.* Stanford, CA: Stanford University Press, 2002.

Jobst, Jack. "Gone Fishing." *Michigan History Magazine* 79 (November/December 1995).

———. "Hemingway at Seney." *Michigan History Magazine* 74 (November/December 1990).

Miller, Madelaine Hemingway, *Ernie: Hemingway's Sister "Sunny" Remembers.* New York: Crown, 1975.

Ohle, William. *How It Was in Horton Bay.* Boyne City, MI: William Ohle, 1989.

———. *100 Years in Horton Bay.* Horton Bay, MI: William Ohle, 1975.

Reynolds, Michael. *The Young Hemingway.* Oxford: Basil Blackwell, 1986.

Sanford, Marcelline Hemingway. *At the Hemingways.* Moscow: University of Idaho Press, 1998.

The Summer Resorts and Waters of Northern Michigan. Chicago: Jones Stationery and Printing, 1884.

The Summer Resorts and Waters of Northern Michigan, Reached via Grand Rapids and Indiana Railroad. Chicago, n.d. [ca. 1886].

Permissions Acknowledgments

Excerpts from Ernest Hemingway letters to C. E. Hemingway (9/19/1917), Howell G. Jenkins (6/16/1919, 7/26/1919, and 9/15/1919), Grace Quinlan (8/8/1920, 7/21/1921, and 8/19/1921), and William B. Smith, Jr. (4/28/1921) reprinted with the permission of Scribner, a division of Simon & Schuster, Inc., from *Ernest Hemingway: Selected Letters, 1917–1961*, edited by Carlos Baker. Copyright © 1981 Ernest Hemingway Foundation, Inc. Copyright outside the United States: © Hemingway Foreign Rights Trust.

Excerpts from unpublished Ernest Hemingway letters to Jim Gamble (4/27/1919) and C. E. Hemingway (6/9/1919, 8/27/1919, and 10/28/1919) printed with the permission of the Ernest Hemingway Foundation and the permission of Scribner, a division of Simon & Schuster, Inc., on behalf of the Hemingway Foreign Rights Trust. Copyright outside the United States: © Hemingway Foreign Rights Trust.

Excerpts from "The Indians Moved Away," "The Last Good Country," "Summer People," "Wedding Day," and "On Writing" reprinted with the permission of Scribner, a division of Simon & Schuster, Inc., from *The Nick Adams Stories* by Ernest Hemingway. Copyright © 1969 by Mary Hemingway. Copyright © 1972, and renewed © 2000 by the Ernest Hemingway Foundation, Inc. Copyright outside the United States: © Hemingway Foreign Rights Trust.

Excerpts from "The End of Something," "Fathers and Sons," "Big Two-Hearted River: Part I," "Big Two-Hearted River: Part II," "Up in Michigan," "The Snows of Kilimanjaro," and "Ten Indians":

In US: Reprinted with the permission of Scribner, a division of Simon & Schuster, Inc., from *The Short Stories of Ernest Hemingway*. Copyright 1925, 1927 by Charles Scribner's Sons. Copyright renewed 1953, 1955 by Ernest Hemingway. Copyright 1933 by Charles Scribner's Sons. Copyright renewed © 1961 by Mary Hemingway. Copyright 1936, 1938 by Ernest Hemingway. Copyright renewed © 1964, 1966 by Mary Hemingway.

In UK: Reprinted from *The First Fortynine Stories* by Ernest Hemingway, published by Jonathan Cape. Reprinted by permission of the Random House Group Ltd.

Excerpts from *A Moveable Feast*:

In US: Reprinted with the permission of Scribner, a division of Simon & Schuster, Inc., from *A Moveable Feast* by Ernest Hemingway. Copyright © 1964 by Mary Hemingway. Copyright renewed © 1992 by John H. Hemingway, Patrick Hemingway, and Gregory Hemingway.

In UK: Reprinted from *A Moveable Feast* by Ernest Hemingway, published by Jonathan Cape. Reprinted by permission of the Random House Group Ltd.

Excerpts from *The Torrents of Spring:*

In US: Reprinted with the permission of Scribner, a division of Simon & Schuster, Inc., from *The Torrents of Spring* by Ernest Hemingway. Copyright 1926 by Charles Scribner's Sons. Copyright renewed 1954 by Ernest Hemingway.

In UK: Excerpts from *The Torrents of Spring* reprinted from *The Torrents of Spring* by Ernest Hemingway, published by Jonathan Cape. Reprinted by permission of the Random House Group Ltd.

INDEX

Page numbers in italics refer to illustrations

Bacon, Elizabeth, *85, 98*
Bacon, Henry, 81, *85, 98*
Bacons' farm, *98–101*
Balmer, Edwin, 172, 178
Bay ferries, 15–18; ticket, *19*
Bay View, xiii, 25
Bolton, Mrs. Nick, *109*
Bolton, Prudence, *109*
Bruce, Toby, 191
Brumback, Ted, 149, 156
Bump, Georgianna, *147, 148,* 174
Bump, Marjorie, *147,* 172, 174, *175*

Charlevoix, xv
Chicago and West Michigan railway, *59*
Clarahan, Lewis, 121, 135, *136, 137*
Clifton House hotel, Petoskey, *42*
Connable, Harriet, 174, *176*
Curtis, Connie, *147*
Cushman, David, 33
Cushman Hotel, *27, 29, 32, 33–35, 47*

Dick, Lucille, *148*
Dilworth, Elizabeth, 140
Dilworth, Jim, 140; blacksmith shop, *143*
Dilworth, Wesley, *131*
Dos Passos, John, 191

Edgar, Carl, 140, *148,* 149, *150, 155,* 184

Fox, Vollie, 142
Fox River, 159, 160, *162, 164*

Gazelle, 17
Goldstein (Gordon), Irene, 174, 191
Grand Rapids and Indiana (GR & I) railroad, 24–33; "dummy trains," *29, 30, 31;* main station, 26–28, *27, 31;* promotional publications, *2, 3, 4, 24;* suburban or "summer" station, *28, 29, 30, 31, 32;* timetable, 1915, *28;* We Que Ton Sing station, *25*
Great Lakes steamships, 8–18

Hall, Ernest, 77; home of in Oak Park, *79*
Hancock, Tyler, *106*
Harbor Point, *19,* 25
Harbor Springs, 19–22; depot, *22;* harbor, *20;* State Street, *21*
Hartwell, Jim, 142
Hemingway, Adelaide, 106, *108*
Hemingway, Anson, 71, 106, *108*
Hemingway, Carol, 68, 78, *103,* 185
Hemingway, Clarence, x, xiii, *49,* 71–73; aboard SS *Manitou, 11;* with Ernest, 1917, *72;* with Ernest and Marcelline, 1901, *73, 120;* at Ernest's wedding, *185, 187;* with Grace at time of marriage, *78;* with his parents, 1914, *79, 108;* letter to Jim Gamble, 1919, *133;* at Longfield Farm, *73, 111, 112;* shooting clay pigeons, *71;* on the SS *State of Ohio,* 1898, *82;* suicide, 71; and Uncle Tyley, *106;* at Windemere, 1920s, *73;* on Windemere beach, 1899, *84*
Hemingway, Ernest: aboard SS *Missouri,* ca. 1916, *14;* canoeing, *123;* with Clarence and Leicester, 1917, *117;* driving sheep, 1900, *100;* fifteenth birthday party, *109;* first birthday, *107;* fishing streams and lakes, *126, 129–35, 138, 169, 170;* with Harold Sampson, 1914, *126;* hiking in Michigan, 135–39; hopping train, 1915 or 1916, *167;* Horton Bay,

148; with Jock Pentecost, 1919, *160;* letters to Clarence Hemingway, 1917,1919, 113, 115, 178; letters to Grace Quinlan, 156, 184, 185–86; letters to Howell Jenkins, 152, 160; letters to Jim Gamble, 145, 151; letter to Bill Smith, 181; living in Petoskey, 1919, 171–78, *176;* at Longfield Farm, 1917, *114;* with Marcelline, Petoskey, *50;* and Michigan, 121–28; *A Moveable Feast,* xvi, 128, 139, 162; *The Nick Adams Stories* (See *The Nick Adams Stories* [Hemingway]); in 1919 after returning from WWI, *159, 163;* in 1921 before his wedding, *182;* at The Pine Barrens, *153, 154, 157, 158, 166, 168;* postcard to father from Seney, *161;* return to Michigan after the War, 149–58; at sixteen, *124;* "The Snows of Kilmanjaro," 101, *193; The Torrents of Spring,* xvi, 23, 52, 57, 193, *194; True at First Light,* 190; "Up in Michigan," 142, 144; at Walloon Lake, *121, 171;* with Warren Sumner, *116;* wedding at Horton Bay, 179–86, *180, 182, 184;* at Windemere, 1905, *122;* with woodchuck, 1916, *127*
Hemingway, Grace (Hall), x, xiii, *49,* 74–76, 77, 81; 1895, *75;* with Clarence at time of marriage, *78;* with Ernest and Marcelline, 1900, *76;* with Ernest at Windemere site, 1899, *83;* at Ernest's wedding, *185, 187;* with Marcelline, 1898, *76*
Hemingway, Leicester, 78, 110, *185*
Hemingway, Madelaine, 68, 76, *103*
Hemingway, Marcelline, x, *50,* 76, 78, *148, 150*
Hemingway, Ursula, 68, 78, *185*
Hemingway family, 77–80; at Bacon's Landing, Walloon Lake, 68; children with coronet, *104;* children at Petoskey, 1906, *6;* children roasting marshmellows, *104;* Clarence, Grace, and Leicester, 1917, *117;* Ernest's wedding, *185;* family at Windemere, *77,*

Hemingway family (*continued*) 87, 91; family portraits, 80; home of in Oak Park, 79; with relatives at Benzonia, 1917, 118
Hopkins, Charles, 149, 154, 155
Horne, Bill, 149, 150, 184
Horton Bay, 13, 140–48, 145, 181; General Store, 142; Red Fox Inn, 142; Stroud's Mill #2, 141
Horton Creek, 131, 145, 146
Horton Point, 144, 145

Irsula of Windemere (rowboat), 74

Jenkins, Howell, 149, 156, 184

Kotesky, John, 179

Lake Charlevoix, 13, 140
Lake Michigan, 13
Little Traverse Bay: and the Bay View dock, 16; ferries, 15–18; tourism promotions publications, 4; view of from Bay View, 17

Manitou, 19
Marcelline of Windemere (rowboat), 94
Menoniqua Beach, 25
Michigan Transit Company routes, 1921, 7

The Nick Adams Stories (Hemingway), ix, xvi; "Big Two-Hearted River," 159, 164, 166, 168, 169, 170; "The End of Something," 141; "Fathers and Sons," 72; "The Last Good Country," 99; "Now I Lay Me," 138; "On Writing," 128, 189; "Summer People," 146, 148; "Ten Indians," 92; "Wedding Day," 188
Northern Michigan Transportation Company, 8
Northland Limited, 26
Northland (steamboat), 19, 20

Ohlsen, Ray, 135
Outing (steamship), 61, 64, 65, 67

Pailthorp, Edwin "Dutch," 172, 174, 176, 184, 191;

Hemingway inscription in copy of *A Farewell to Arms*, 192
Pennsylvania Park, 33, 35
Pentecost, Jock, 156, 159, 160, 184
Pere Marquette railroad depot, 53, 58; electric trolley running from station to Bay View, 58
Petoskey, xiii, xiv, xv, 23–60; Arlington Hotel, 27, 36–38; breakwater, 53, 54, 56, 57; City Park Grill, 30, 34, 47; D. N. White Bakery, 45; Fochtman's Department Store, 50, 51; hotels, 33–43; Lake Street, 46; McCarthy's Barbershop, 51; The Midway, 48; Mitchell Street, 48, 52; National Hotel, 43; New Arlington Hotel, 37, 38; Oriental Hotel, 43; Park House hotel, 41; The Perry (Hotel Perry), 39–40; Petoskey High School, 175; Public Library building, 177; railroads, 24–32; street scenes, 44–52; turn-of-century tourists in, 5; typical road, ca. 1915, 116; waterfront, 53–57
Petoskey Boat Company, 56
Petoskey Evening News: November 12, 1919, 177; September 27, 1947, 192; September 1921, 187
Pine Barrens, 150, 152, 153, 157
Pinehurst Cottage, Horton Bay, 140, 144, 147, 186
Potter, Eva, boardinghouse, 172, 173

Quinlan, Grace, 172, 174, 179

Ramsdell, Luman, 172, 174, 184
Rapid Transit (steamship), 61
Reycroft, John and George, 39
Richardson, Hadley, 179, 183, 189
Roaring Brook, Little Traverse Bay, 25
Rose, Hiram, 36

Sampson, Harold, 121
Search Light, 15
Seney, 159–70; Grondin Hotel, 165
Silver Spray (ferry), 15
Sly, Helen, 147
Smale, Dick, 156
Smith, Bill, 121, 140, 149, 150, 151, 152, 154, 155, 156, 172, 184

Smith, Katy, 121, 140, 148, 150, 179, 191
Smith, Y. K., 179
SS *Manitou*, 6, 9, 12; Chicago newspaper advertisement for, 10; Clarence Hemingway aboard, 1920s, 11; deck plans, 1916, 10; at Harbor Springs, 20; passing lighthouse at Harbor Point, 20; ticket, 11
SS *Missouri*, 13, 14, 136, 147; Ernest Hemingway aboard, ca. 1916, 14
Stroud, Alanzo, home, 143
Sturgeon River, 181
Summer Resorts and Waters of Northern Michigan, 5
Sumner, Warren, 110, 113, 114, 115
Sunny (launch boat), 94

Tourist (steamship), 61, 64, 65, 66

Ursula of Windemere, 94; family photo in, 95

Vernon (ferry), 17
Von Kurowsky, Agnes, 149

Walker, Al, 159, 160
Walloon Lake and village, 61–68; Bacon's Landing, 67, 68; Echo Beach Inn, 67; Haynes Boat Livery, 63; Merrill Boat Livery, 64; The New Walloon (hotel), 63; Walloon Lake (formerly Bear Lake), xiii, 53, 54, 56, 57, 62, 67, 81, 84; Walloon rail station, 62; Walloon village, 62
Wequetonsing, 16, 25
Windemere Cottage, xiii, 81–92; completed, 1900, 86; during construction, 1899, 84, 86; fireplace, 88; interior, ca. 1900, 89, 90; kitchen wing addition, 1902, 87; and Walloon Lake, 88, 91, 92
Windemere Cottage, summers at, 93–118; Bacons' farm, 98–101; diversions, 102–5; "Grace Cottage," 110, 115; guests, 106–9; letters to and from, 105; Longfield Farm, 110–15; road trip from Oak Park, 116–18; on and in the water, 94–97